Myth-makers and Story-tellers

Myth-makers and Story-tellers

How to unleash the power of Myths, Stories and Metaphors to understand the past, envisage the future, and create lasting and positive cultural change in your organisation

❀ Michael Kaye ❀

Business & Professional Publishing

First published 1996
by Business & Professional Publishing Pty Ltd
Level 7, 10 Help Street, Chatswood, Sydney, NSW 2067 Australia
Phone: (02) 415 1548 Fax: (02) 419 2948

© Michael Kaye 1996

ISBN 1 875680 26 8

All rights reserved. Apart from any fair dealing for the purposes of study, research or review, as permitted under Australian copyright law, no part of this book may be reproduced by any means without the written permission of the publisher.

The National Library of Australia
Cataloguing-in-Publication entry

Kaye, Michael, 1940-.
   Myth-makers and story-tellers: How to unleash the power of myths,
   stories and metaphors to understand the past, envisage the future,
   and create lasting and positive cultural changes in your organization.

Bibliography.
Includes index.
ISBN 1 875680 26 8.

1. Communication in organizations. 2. Corporate culture.
3. Management. I. Title.

658.45

Cover design by Drawing A Living
Printed in Australia by Ligare Pty Ltd

This book is dedicated to all managers who believe it is
important to reflect on their work practices and who
are constantly looking for new perspectives
for understanding and influencing
organisational life

Foreword

As the managing director of a rapidly growing high-technology company I am faced daily with a bewildering range of issues that require my attention. In order to do my job most effectively in the limited time available, I must identify and address those issues that will maximise the success of our company. These issues must be those that give us the most leverage in positively influencing the business life of the company.

Over the last few years I have come to realise that an important feature of the business, which can be a source of enormous leverage for me and my management team, is the culture of the company. An appropriate corporate culture is one that facilitates the achievement of corporate goals. Such a culture helps management much like a tidal surge, by lifting the entire company up and over many barriers to success. An inappropriate culture, like a receding tide, can leave management high and dry, without the necessary support of the company.

I believe that good managers have always been aware of this, even if only subliminally. They have heavily influenced their corporate cultures by contributing to and pruning the store of myths and stories that have defined their corporate cultures.

As with managing any other aspect of a business, it is first necessary to understand your company's culture before you can manage it effectively. It was while Object Oriented Pty Ltd was trying to understand and describe its corporate culture that we heard of Michael's work and sought his help. We find Michael's ideas very useful in helping us understand our corporate culture. We have come to recognise myths and story-listening as powerful means of understanding our corporate culture.

Foreword

Our current project is to formulate strategies for managing the further evolution of our corporate culture. We are hoping to use myths and storytelling to positively influence this evolution—to create a culture that facilitates better communication and is fully supportive of our corporate goals.

I have personally found Michael's ideas in *Myth-makers and Story-tellers* valuable in helping me and my management team to understand the definition and evolution of an appropriate corporate culture using myths and stories. I unreservedly recommend it as essential reading for managers of all businesses employing more than two or three people.

–Gerry Carroll
Managing Director
Object Oriented Pty Ltd

Contents

Foreword   vii
Preface   xiii
About the author   xvii
Introduction   xix

Part I: Communicating through stories

1   TELLING STORIES IN EVERYDAY LIFE   3

Why learn about stories?   3
Why do people tell stories?   5
What types of stories do people tell?   8
How are people influenced by stories?   16
Summary   21

2   THE STORY-TELLING ORGANISATION   23

What is a story-telling organisation?   23
Why do people in organisations tell stories?   25
What are organisational stories about?   30
Who are the story-tellers in organisations?   33
How are stories communicated?   35
Story-telling skills   39
Story-listening skills   45
Summary   49

Contents

Part II: The organisational myth

3 THE NATURE AND PURPOSE OF ORGANISATIONAL MYTHS 53

The nature of myth   55
What are organisational myths?   57
Why do myths exist in organisations?   63
Sources of organisational myths   68
Summary   74

4 THEMES, ARCHETYPES, HEROES AND METAPHORS 75

Themes in organisational myths   75
Archetypes   86
Heroes   91
The language of organisational myths—metaphor   97
Summary   104

Part III: Building the story-telling organisation

5 CREATING AND CHANGING ORGANISATIONAL CULTURE 107

What is organisational culture?   107
Building a culture with myth and story   117
Managing change through story-telling   122
The shadow side and covert culture   126
Creating a positive organisational culture   132
Summary   137

Contents

6   DEVELOPING THE ART OF STORY-TELLING   138

Managers as story-tellers and story-listeners   138
An approach for training managers   147
Consultants as story-tellers and story-listeners   159
Professional development for consultants   165
Summary   169

7   ORGANISATIONAL STORY-TELLERS OF TOMORROW   170

The story-telling organisation of tomorrow   170
Story-telling competencies for tomorrow's managers   173
Monitoring cultural change and differences   182
Preparing to 'buck the system'   184
Summary   186

Endnotes   187
Index   195

Preface

During the past couple of years, I have been amazed over and over again at the growing number of managers who become excited when a new view of their professional world is opened up to them. In particular, many human resource development managers with whom I have been associated professionally and academically have been intrigued by the power of their organisation's myths and stories to influence learning, change and innovation. Over the last decade, at the University of Technology, Sydney (UTS), alone, some thousands of managers have completed a graduate major in communication management—a field of study which includes story-telling and organisational myths as an integral part of its theoretical foundations. More and more managers undertaking UTS graduate courses in communication management are cultivating story-telling as an area for independent study and research.

My enthusiasm for the study of organisational myths and story-telling grew, in part, from the buzzing interest of these managers, but was also sharpened by the fascinating work of leading contemporary scholars like David Boje, whose published work on story-telling has had a significant impact on my thinking. I have not used a conventional academic textbook style in *Myth-makers and Story-tellers,* which is, I believe, very much in line with the direction of many other applied social science scholars. One recurrent point in *Myth-makers and Story-tellers* is the repeated discovery of managers' and educators' disillusionment with the familiar, conventional and simplistic 'how to do it' literature on management practice and organisational behaviour.

There is probably a good deal of commonsense in practical management books. Nevertheless, increasing numbers of today's managers and management educators want more. Not only do they want to know the few easy steps for doing something, they want to know why those steps are the best or most appropriate ones. Kurt Lewin's claim that 'there is nothing as practical as a good theory' finally seems to have found its mark in many of today's organisations. In this book, story-telling is presented as one applied theoretical perspective for helping managers gain deeper insights into their professional worlds. With new ways of understanding organisational life and culture, managers will have a basis for lifelong learning in the workplace and for planning and implementing innovation and change.

One assumption on which this book rests, therefore, is that theory cannot be separated from practice. I've blended the thinking of contemporary scholars with everyday examples of organisational communication and behaviour. The case studies in this book are all based on true real-life incidents or events. In many instances, they derive from the author's personal experiences in organisations. For reasons which are obvious, many of the organisations or the people involved cannot be identified. You will appreciate the sensitivity of some of the stories of blundering or unthinking managerial practices and the risk I would be taking to expose the anti-heroes, villains and professional failures I have protectively described throughout this book. Of course, wherever possible, I have identified the organisation and the people in the story.

Integration of theory and practice is also evident in the focus on training and development managers and organisational development consultants as story-tellers. I didn't want the reader to travel through the tantalising world of myth and story-telling only to find that at the journey's end there was nowhere else to go. The book does provide practical suggestions for continued self-development in story-telling and self-directed lifelong learning about making life in organisations stimulating, challenging and rewarding. For this reason, there is an emphasis on adult learning principles and goals as a focus for the professional development of managers and organisational development consultants in the story-telling organisation.

Using both the thinking of today's scholars and best management practices in organisations, I have given my vision of tomorrow's story-telling organisation and the abilities future managers will need to have to be successful story-tellers and listeners. I have no doubt that as I continue to venture into unexplored parts of the world of myth, my vision will become more elaborate.

Preface

It is hard to imagine anyone who gets caught up in myth-making and myth-interpretation not being tempted to speculate on the future. Myths can help us do that because they enable us to become attuned to a timeless existence. Yesterday's stories are still relevant today and are likely to be told again in the future.

I have intended this book as a resource for the 'thinking manager'—which means just about any manager committed to communicative excellence and good working relationships with staff. It will also appeal to 'general readers' who may be enticed to mythologise their interpersonal experiences as a way of making better sense of their working lives. Certainly, management educators, trainers, human resource developers and organisational development consultants will be able to apply the ideas and suggestions in this book in their professional practice. Broadly speaking, *Myth-makers and Story-tellers* will benefit those who recognise that they are lifelong learners and who are committed to learning from the myths and stories available to them in their organisational lives.

About the author

Michael Kaye, PhD (Macquarie University) is an Associate Professor in Adult Education at the University of Technology, Sydney (UTS). Until July 1994, he was Head of School of Adult Vocational Education. Prior to that, he was Head of the Department of Communication Studies at Kuring-gai College of Advanced Education. He is the author of *Communication Management*, published in 1994 by Prentice Hall, and has written numerous journal articles and book chapters on communication, management and education. He has also presented many papers at international and national academic and professional conferences. At the 1994 Australian and New Zealand Academy of Management Conference Michael Kaye was awarded the Best Paper Prize for his paper on Organisational Myths, Story-telling and Communication Management.

Since 1991, Michael Kaye has co-ordinated a major subject sequence on Adult Communication Management in the Master of Education in Adult Education at UTS. In addition to 30 years of experience as a teacher and scholar, Michael Kaye has had considerable experience as a management and organisation development consultant to private and public organisations in Australia. His particular areas of expertise in his consulting work centre on communication management in organisations, with emphasis on developing the communicative competence of managers, including their creative and critical thinking abilities. In 1994, Michael became a director of Gilpin & Kaye Pty Ltd—a company with associates who are specialist organisational development consultants to international and local organisations.

Introduction

Every day we are confronted with stories of different kinds. We read newspaper stories, we hear tales of woe or triumph from those we know and work with, and we learn of heroic deeds performed by people of distinction or public figures. A 'story', therefore, is best thought of in its broadest sense—as narrated or written information that enriches our understanding of the world and of the people who affect our lives. In some cases, stories endure for a long time—partly because of their striking or dramatic qualities but also partly because they become closely identified with the culture of the system where they are heard and told. These kinds of stories are the myths that guide our thinking, communication and actions in our daily lives.

Truth and fantasy

Organisational myths tell us about heroes and life in human systems. As we hear or read each new story, we extend our focal range for seeing our organisations as they really are. Every myth serves to magnify our vision. Our capacity to understand is enhanced by the zoom and wide-angle lenses myths give to our eyes. What we learn from myths is true—but the myths themselves may not always reflect reality. Just as many organisational myths are based on truths, there are also myths that are based on highly questionable premises and assumptions. Errors of reasoning must be teased out in order to arrive at the point where the myth can be a valuable learning tool and can assist in

Introduction

developing illuminating insights into the world of communication and interpersonal relationships.

For example, some managers believe that the time spent on a task is the best indicator of how hard their staff are working. The assumption behind this myth can be questioned—can people spend a lot of time at work doing precious little? Yes, they can, and this means that the discovery here is a truth about an unreality or a false belief. Spending time examining the values or myths of an organisation can reveal such false beliefs.

Nevertheless, it is important to disown the popular idea that myths are, by definition, statements of falsehood. 'Myth' should not be simply equated with lies, deception, fiction or fantasy. In our everyday conversations we do tend to use the word 'myth' in this way. For example, we may say it is wishful thinking or a 'myth' that in contemporary Western society successful and amicable enterprise agreements will ever be made between employers and employees or that politicians are socially conscious and responsible people—not opportunists. The story-telling organisation's myths, however, are not mere flights of fantasy but traditionally and historically captured slices of life.

Although in popular terms we may think of myths being fiction disguised as truth, the heroes of famous organisational myths did actually carry out their valorous exploits. In the 1980s, Jack Welch and his executive team at General Electric made brilliant strategic decisions to make the organisation the market leader in every product division. More recently, in 1991, Roger Michaelsen succeeded in creating a positive team culture at the Kodak Customer Assistance Center in Rochester, New York. Kerry Packer and Rupert Murdoch have now become part of the mythology surrounding the struggle between the Super League movement and the established Australian Rugby League system. This struggle has been so intense and prolonged that its stories are assuming epic proportions. In effect, the myths relating to the rise of the Super League seem only the beginning of a continuing saga.

If organisational stories were only figments of people's imaginations, they would not give us life-scripts and we would not have a basis for learning from them. We experience the reality of our worlds through all the stories we hear and read in our organisations. Many of these stories are myths built around heroes and archetypes who guide us in our thinking, communication and actions. Myths are very much part of our real working world. In a world without myths, we would become like the 'technologised' people of Aldous Huxley's *Brave New World* who substituted the tranquilliser 'soma' for thinking and learning. Fortunately, we still have organisational myths even though there is the danger that our professional worlds are becoming gradually demythologised. It is in our own best interests to ensure that we nurture and preserve our organisational mythologies.

Overview of the book

In Part I we begin our journey into the intriguing world of story and myth. Our exploration will show us that all kinds of stories are part of our everyday lives. They enable us not only to share information and feelings—to communicate—but also to learn from our experiences. In our daily lives, stories are vehicles for lifelong learning, as well as the basis for managing our communication processes. Thus, in Chapter 1, we ask the foundation questions: 'Why learn about stories?', 'Why do people tell stories?', 'What kinds of stories do people tell?' and 'How are people influenced by stories?'.

Following the introduction to a story-telling world in Chapter 1, Chapter 2 narrows our focus to 'the story-telling organisation'. We ask what a story-telling organisation is and why stories are told in organisations. As we look closely at what happens in the story-telling organisation, we'll discover who the story-tellers are and how they communicate. We'll also identify the kinds of skills people need to be successful story-tellers and story-listeners. Finally, we'll examine the sorts of things organisational stories are about.

Part II focuses on organisational myths. In Chapter 3, we'll be asking what organisational myths are and why they exist. As well, we'll be asking how organisational myths are created and who their creators are. Then we'll look at some of the kinds of myths which typically arise and develop in organisations.

Our delving into the world of organisational myths is extended in Chapter 4 where we unmask common themes in the story-telling organisation. Closely linked with this is the identification of archetypes in organisational myths. We'll see how archetypes can eventually become heroic role-models for people in organisations. In addition to learning about the characters in organisational stories, we'll find out some of the typical plots of the stories in which heroes have played their parts. In the concluding section, we'll explore the language of organisational myths, looking particularly at the kinds of symbols and metaphors which are frequently used to describe managerial and organisational practices.

Our journey takes us, in Part III, along the path to building the story-telling organisation. The two complementary themes here are changing old cultures and building positive new cultures. Chapter 5 turns our thinking to the contribution of myths and story-telling to organisational culture. We ask what 'organisational culture' means, and how we can change an organisation's culture through story-telling. Here, in particular, we'll focus on two issues: how to manage the 'shadow side' of organisational culture and how to build a positive organisational culture by telling and listening to stories.

Practical considerations for training managers and organisational development consultants to be good story-tellers and story-listeners occupy us in Chapter 6. We'll discuss an approach for training and developing managers and in so doing match this with the skills they will need to possess. Similarly, we'll describe and analyse an approach to train and develop consultants to be professionally skilled in auditing organisations through the interpretation of stories.

Chapter 7 looks to the future. If story-telling is a critical part of communication competence, how will the stories of tomorrow and the ways they are told be different from today's stories? We ask what kinds of new skills will tomorrow's managers need to carry out their likely future roles successfully? Some of our attention will be given to skills like impromptu story-telling, creative story-telling, thinking in metaphors and critical listening. We'll conclude by suggesting how the external environment and the internal culture of organisations will need to change to truly foster and encourage better communication through story-telling.

I

communicating
through stories

1

telling stories in everyday life

The difference between a poor and a good story is—one you hear; the other you tell.
F. J. Mills, *'The Twinkler' in* Dinkum Oil *(1917)*

What's the point of a book about stories? In this chapter we learn how stories are fragments of life and that the understanding and management of our personal and professional worlds is bound up with our sharing of stories with other people. We'll learn that stories map for us acceptable ways of communicating and acting. We'll find out why people tell stories and what kinds of stories we hear and tell in our daily lives. Finally, we'll explore how stories can influence people to change their attitudes. We'll discover that with a greater understanding through sharing stories, people can establish new and different ways of communicating successfully with others.

Why learn about stories?

'There are eight million stories in the Naked City. This has been just one of them.' These words concluded every episode of 'The Naked City', a very popular television series in the 1960s. All the inhabitants of the Naked City

Part I: Communicating through stories

had experiences that eventually became stories to be remembered and told. By sharing stories about themselves and others, they learned about life in their community and their world of work. This kind of learning helped individuals in the Naked City to develop significant personal and professional relationships. People's lives became enriched when they communicated through the telling and hearing of stories.

Communication is like breathing—you have to breathe in order to live. *How* we breathe determines the quality of our life. If we are aerobically unfit, our breathing may be shallow, coming in short gasps for air when we are physically exhausted. On the other hand, if we are in good shape, our breathing is deeper and more measured. So, we can breathe easily or we can breathe with difficulty, depending on our state of health.

Our communication, like our breathing, indicates something about our state of health. If our stories are unimaginative, uninteresting and lacking in vitality, we communicate the fact that we have not learned or changed as a result of our life experiences. In a sense, stories are 'quality of life meters'. They are measures of how well attuned we are to our world and of the extent to which we eagerly seize every opportunity to learn from our life experiences. Zorba the Greek, a literary role model for zestful living, epitomised the type of person whose story-telling gifts enriched his own and others' lives. Despite not having many material possessions or riches, and despite financial and personal setbacks from time to time, Zorba still found joy and exhilaration in every moment of his life. This love of life was expressed through the stories he told everyone, including the conservative Englishman he befriended.

Gaining meaning from our life experiences, therefore, enables us to tell stories that signal to others how happy we are with our lot and how in tune we are with our world. At any stage of our lives, our stories reflect our state of harmony or disharmony with our environment. We learn to communicate in very basic ways from the time we are born. As we mature and develop, our 'stories' become more sophisticated. Our ways of communicating change throughout our lifelong learning process. People who benefit and learn from their experience of life enrich their communication with others. They have more stories to tell. Others, failing to take advantage of learning opportunities, don't appear to change much. How often have we encountered adults who still talk and act like children?

People who have lots of stories to tell give added value to their personal and professional relationships. These people do not tell the same story over and over again and they can readily detect if their listeners are tuning out. As George Jessel once said, 'If you haven't struck oil in your first three minutes, stop boring!'. Good story-tellers, then, are also competent communicators—they can sense if their stories are being well received or not. Good story-tellers use audience feedback to modify the way they communicate their stories. So, learning and communicating through story-telling and story-listening are processes we need to understand and manage well if we want to have satisfying and rewarding lifestyles.

Why do people tell stories?

From early childhood, stories become an important part of our lives. Parents read bedtime stories to their children. The stories can be as short as a brief incident captured in a nursery rhyme or they can be longer, like fairy tales. Major movies have given an even greater exposure to well known stories like *Snow White and the Seven Dwarfs*, *Aladdin*, *Ali Baba and the 40 Thieves*, *Peter Pan*, *Huckleberry Finn*, *Emil and the Detectives* and Rudyard Kipling's *Jungle Book*. There are now many forms in which classic stories from the creative minds of people like Hans Christian Anderson, the Brothers Grimm and Aesop are published or distributed—as comics or movies or video games, as well as standard children's books.

One powerful reason for parents telling children stories is that the story-telling event strengthens the parent-child relationship. The fact that parents take the time to read stories to their children suggests that they enjoy the company of their children. As much as anything, parents love to see their children's looks of wonder as new stories are told, new learning occurs and new experiences of life are savoured. It can be an emotional time when stories create strong feelings and family ties. Of course, parents may also read stories to instruct their children. Many children's stories feature a moral or teaching point, often about basic survival, healthy living or getting on well with other people. In Robert Louis Stevenson's *Treasure Island*, Jim Hawkins,

Part I: Communicating through stories

the young cabin boy on the *Hispaniola*, not only shows courage but also learns that discretion is the better part of valour when the ship falls under the control of mutineering pirates.

As adults, we also read and listen to stories which can teach us something. In management development courses, for instance, the case study is an effective kind of instructional story. Usually, the case study is about a manager who managed something or somebody well or poorly. In training rooms, the story is usually discussed by participants, who are encouraged to draw conclusions about actions leading to 'best practice'. Typical examples of case studies for advanced management training can be found in Kenneth Blanchard and Spencer Johnson's book, *The One Minute Manager*.[1]

Nevertheless, we should not develop the impression that adults learn from stories only in formal training sessions. The stories told informally in cafeterias, bars, staff loungerooms and in corridors can serve as powerful lessons on how we should act or communicate in work situations.

Often the stories we hear in conversations at work are about people who have made a difference or contribution to the organisation. There are stories about memorable employees and managers of the past and present, just as there are stories about people who have blundered or committed misdemeanours. Similarly, there are stories about organisational events like Christmas parties, office picnics, the annual ball, farewell dinners and other social and official functions when members have shared recollections of vivid and sometimes humorous occurrences. 'Who can forget the time when . . . ' are the words which often start the telling or retelling of such stories.

There are several other reasons for people to tell stories, which will be examined more closely in the next chapter. Essentially, reasons for telling a story depend a lot on the direction of our communicative goals. Roger Schank has identified three categories of story-telling goals: *me-goals*, *you-goals* and *conversational goals*.[2] People who have 'me-goals' tell stories that are typically self-centred. Often, me-goal directed stories are told by individuals who need to give vent to their feelings, so story-telling is a bit like letting off steam.

'You-goal' stories are about people other than the story-teller and are intended for the benefit of others. These stories are told to make a specific point, to provoke feelings in the listener, to inspire, to publicise information and to summarise important happenings. Many you-goal oriented stories are told when the story-teller has strong feelings or views about something. For this reason, effective narrators of you-goal stories are likely to have well-developed persuasion skills as part of their repertoire of communicative abilities.

People with conversational goals tell stories because they want the dialogue between themselves and their listeners to be kept as open as possible, so that the conversation and thus the relationship will not die. Stories with conversational goals relate to both teller and listener. Question-and-answer sequences are good examples of conversational goal stories, since questioners usually expect stories for answers. These answers are usually like a story precis—capable of being elaborated into a more detailed account. Instances where this happens are easily found:

> Q: So what did you do when your job was declared redundant?
> A: I did what I always wanted to do and started my own consulting business.
>
> Q: Where did you go after you left her apartment last night?
> A: I went to my hotel and had a nightcap in the club lounge.
>
> Q: Were there any witnesses at the time of the accident?
> A: Two Salvation Army Officers saw what happened. I took their names and addresses.

In each instance, the answer implicitly carries the further solicitation 'Why don't you ask me some more?'.

Consider how often we use the actual word 'story' when we ask people questions. Do any of these sound familiar?

> - Okay, so you're late. What's your story?
> - Yeah, it didn't work out. Story of your life. Want to tell me about it?
> - Same old story—I applied but missed out for lack of experience.
> - A likely story! You expect me to believe that?
> - So, let's go back over your story. What happened when you first got there?

Part I: Communicating through stories

What types of stories do people tell?

Obviously, the word 'story' can mean different things depending on how it is used—an excuse, a tale of woe, deceit and lying, or a verbal recounting of some incident. Nevertheless, all these meanings can be legitimately applied to the process of story-telling in our daily lives.

While we do clearly tend to refer to 'stories' in our everyday vocabulary, we can also note that the word 'story' is often cited in quite specific contexts. For instance, we often hear references to 'newspaper stories', 'war stories', 'police stories' or 'sports stories'. Mostly, these stories refer to journalistic accounts of specific events, individuals and their achievements. Sometimes in special circumstances references are made in the singular, as in 'the accused's story'. In the movie world, the film of the life of Moses has been described as the 'greatest story ever told'. And in the field of medicine, general practitioners relate the story or history of a patient through letters of referral to specialist doctors.

Perhaps the most significant reason for story-telling is that the process enables us to experience our world with greater understanding. Speaking about the power of stories on the daily lives of people, the noted scholar of mythology Joseph Campbell observed that 'we tell stories to try to come to terms with the world, to harmonise our lives with reality'.[3] Campbell saw story-telling as a way of putting people's minds in touch with 'the experience of being alive'. Thus, many stories become role models for developing a satisfying and fulfilling lifestyle. For example, stories of courageous individuals overcoming adversity or handicaps often serve to make others realise just how fortunate they are.

What types of stories do people tell and listen to? The simple answer is—all kinds of stories. Some people revel in recounting to others detailed stories of their state of physical health. Others like to talk about their work or their latest achievements. There are those who like to give their interpretations of current political or industrial happenings. Close friends share private stories about themselves and others who matter in their lives. All these are stories of one kind or another in our daily lives and we hear them often.

The urban myth

Among the more bizarre tales becoming part of everyday life are urban legends or modern myths. Generally, these stories have no basis of truth but, when told by skilful narrators, 'can be so convincing that police and the media are often snared in the hype and frenzy whipped up around them'.[4] One of the best known urban myths is the story of a female hitchhiker who is driven home by two men. As she gets out of the car, she tells the men they are welcome to drop in any time if they are passing by. The next day the men return to the house, only to learn that the hitchhiker had been killed some years ago in a car crash, exactly where the two men picked her up the previous day.

Most of the stories we hear every day, however, do not have this strange, twisted, 'Twilight Zone' touch to them. Our everyday stories are typically brief and do not survive to become legends or myths.

Untold stories

Of course, there are stories people know but are not readily prepared to disclose. People who are having secret love affairs or who are concealing some malicious act or evil intent are highly unlikely to share such information even with their closest confidants. Untold stories, however, like openly known stories, can influence the behaviour and communication of their owners. This is because stories in some ways are like 'life scripts'. They provide us with a map of how to go about our daily tasks and routines. We will refer to the notion of 'life script' from time to time thoughout *Myth-makers and Storytellers*. At this point, however, it is enough to say that our lifetime can be likened to a continuous play with many acts, which are performed according to the stories we adopt and those others script for us. People perform some of their acts to restricted audiences and the scripts remain known only to those who will not judge harshly the morality of the story in question.

Gossip

Many of the stories we hear in everyday life are created through gossip. Some of the kinds of words that usually introduce such stories are:

> - Whatever happened to Thomas when he passed out?
> - I have to tell you what that manager said to her executive assistant!
> - Can you believe the staff's reaction to Joe's pep talk?
> - Didn't Marcus really make a muck of it at today's stockholders' meeting?
> - Is it true the boss and Trudy were caught necking in the car park after work?

Gossip is very common in human systems, regardless of whether these are work organisations or social networks like a sporting club or a local community service centre. Through our conversations with friends, relatives, neighbours and other acquaintances we discover which couples are separating, seeking divorce, engaged or getting married, who is sleeping with whom, who has lost a job, who is ill or dying, and who has done something to become famous or infamous. People are naturally curious about others they know or have heard about and their curiosity is bound to generate speculations which when corroborated turn into stories. Unfounded gossip, on the other hand, can lead to rumours. If rumours remain unchecked, they may seriously damage people's reputations and credibility.

The media

Outside our personal lives, we have access to many human interest stories through the various media. Almost every day, there are tragic accounts of individuals in our community being killed or maimed. There are endless stories about the rise and fall of politicians or entrepreneurs, of millionaires going bankrupt, of celebrities' private lives and experiences, and of heroes and heroines working tirelessly for the benefit of less fortunate or capable folk. Often these stories come to media consumers as prominent journalists' interpreted digests of events and people's actions—the truth or accuracy of a news story may be only partially revealed because of the reporter's slant.

Nevertheless, there are many news stories that cannot be tampered with. For example, the annual reporting of the Australia Day and Queen's Birthday Honours Lists is factual and not subject to any interpretation: 'Ms Betty Gwynne was awarded an Order of Australia Medal for services to the community or to industry.' Stories about accidents and disasters are also usually factual: 'Three people were killed in a head-on collision between two cars', or 'Seventy-nine passengers and crew perished in the crash of a 727 airliner.' Similarly, the Pope's annual Christmas message can be heard firsthand from the Vatican without any massaging from news reporters. Factual stories like these have a 'bottom line' that is unequivocal and not subject to various interpretations.

A script for conduct

In our own professional and personal worlds, there are also many factual stories. For example, we learn factual stories about our local community and municipal council through annual reports, financial statements and new policy announcements. If we join a club, we are given the rules of membership, such as rules about acceptable attire in dining and lounge areas. Similarly, when we join a professional society, we can expect to receive a constitution and articles of association. These membership rules and articles of association are our 'scripts' for appropriate communication and conduct.

Nearly everywhere we go daily, we will be given explicit scripts. In most shops and department stores, for instance, we learn that it is not acceptable to smoke or to consume food or drink on the premises. In a library, we follow the 'script' of not holding loud conversations that could disturb nearby readers. In banks or other financial institutions, we wait in line or queues to be served. Likewise, in many restaurants the sign near the entrance often states 'Please wait here to be seated'. So, in a substantial part of our daily lives, we have a pretty good idea of the scripts and stories which teach us how we are expected to communicate and act in various situations and circumstances.

Most official stories of these kinds are clear and unambiguous. They do not, however, guarantee that people will follow the expected script. People still park their cars in the Disabled Parking zone or smoke in prohibited areas. Paper wrappings are still dropped on streets and footpaths rather than put into litter bins. On parliamentary election days, people forget to vote, even though they have been given reminders on leaflets in their letterboxes, on radio and on television. In such cases, the stories exist but their scripts are ignored.

Second-hand stories

The stories we have talked about so far are part of our society's culture. Everybody knows these kinds of stories although some will deviate from their

Part I: Communicating through stories

scripts. Other stories reach us second-hand. When we hear second-hand stories we have no way of being absolutely sure whether they are true or fabrications. In ancient times, some epic stories like Homer's *Iliad* or *Odyssey* were handed down orally from generation to generation. There is good reason to suppose that after hundreds of years of retelling the stories the latest version differs in some distinctive ways from the original narration. Some details have probably disappeared, new information might have been introduced and old details changed. Even in the shorter, compressed story-telling sequences typical in organisational life, this happens. There is a simple way to demonstrate this. Read the following story aloud to someone else.

> The national sales manager of a large manufacturing company, Hugh Byum, expressed his concern to the youthful sales team that nationwide sales of the newest product, a portable TV alarm clock, had failed to reach projected target figures in September 1995 by an estimated $A1.2 million. Although the recommended retail price of the portable TV alarm clock was reckoned by the company's marketing adviser, Sellam Deare, to be $A325 when the product was launched on 23 November 1994, it was evident that mainly duty-free shoppers were prepared to buy the TV alarm clock. No doubt this was because this item sold for less than $A260 in some duty-free shops. It also appeared that male executives under 30 years of age were the most frequent buyers. Many major local distributors, like Budget Electronics and A-V Enterprises, have attributed the poor sales of this product to its high price and the perception of it as a luxury item. One prominent economist, Professor Itter (commonly known as Prof. Itter), thinks the product may have been overpriced by $A50, while a technical expert writing for *Choice* magazine, Charlie Foxtrot, claims the problem is that travellers would be reluctant to spend money on something which would have little use each day beyond programming wake-up calls.

When you have finished, ask your listener to tell this story to another person. Be sure you are present when your listener is recounting the story. This should ideally be repeated three or four times—in other words, the story should be retold four or five times. What changes to the story can you notice with each retelling? What details become blurred? Do amounts and numbers change? Is the sequence of events kept intact from one retelling to the next?

The truth is that story-telling is an art requiring creative talent and imagination. Story-tellers take pride in adding their own 'spice' to the stories and yarns they concoct or recount. Very skilful story-tellers make adaptations to suit different audiences. Even second-hand stories can have an inventive element—'When I retell it, I'll add a bit about X to make it more appealing'. What we may not realise is that in our retelling of the story, we'll also be making some changes without really being aware that we are doing so.

'Unofficial' stories

When different versions of a story are heard and told in the same setting, people tend to separate what they think is the 'official' story from other 'unofficial' stories. Official stories are usually told by credible, authoritative sources and are very often, but not necessarily, first-hand accounts.

If we can imagine a challenge to the leadership of the Utopian Products board as the main event of a story, the various versions of the story might go something like this:

> Mr I. M. Wright, secretary and executive officer to the Board: 'The challenger, Ms Oyl Wynn, received 12 votes. The current presiding member, Mr Will Stay, gained five votes. I declare Ms Wynn the new chair of the board.' (A possible 'official' story.)
>
> Mr Hugh L. Stryke, union organiser: 'Will Stay was the victim of a conspiracy by ambitious schemers to remove him from the helm. At least he had a few loyal supporters who voted for him.' (An 'unofficial' account. That Stay was voted out is correct but the existence of a conspiracy is conjectural. Emotive words like 'ambitious schemers' also detract from the veracity of the story.)
>
> Ms A. Fairgogh, the equal employment opportunity officer: 'Oyl Wynn was clearly the better candidate for the job, as the majority of discerning voters decided. The company will benefit from new blood at the top. Conservative men like Stay have to go, as the company's image is not as good as it could have been under a more vital person's leadership.' (Another 'unofficial' story with embellishments, such as her allusions to 'discerning voters' and 'a more vital person's leadership' which were not part of the official script. The reference to 'conservative men' also suggests a bias in favour of a female candidate.)

Part I: Communicating through stories

> Mr Will Stay, previous Chair: 'I congratulate Ms Wynn and wish her the very best for her new role in the company. Smart bookmakers would have given odds of 12 to five that she would be victorious. I thank those fellow board members who voted for me and who continue to see me playing a useful role in this company.' (This is also an 'unofficial' story told by the former chair, trying to give the impression of being a gracious loser but betraying his real feelings by implying that some members of the board no longer see him playing a useful role in the company.)
>
> Ms Oyl Wynn, the new company Chair: 'I want to thank all those board members who showed the confidence to elect me to this position. I will do everything possible to justify their trust in my ability to lead the organisation and to use the excellent foundations laid by my predecessor as a starting point for getting this company to be number one market leader.' (Yet another 'unofficial' story. It hints at the weakness of the former chair by projecting an aggressive business leader image.)

The report from I. M. Wright is our most likely 'official' story based on fact. The secretary counted the votes. In each alternative version of this story, there is an element of truth. The introduction of evaluative words and phrases, however, tends to slant the story towards a particular point of view. Stryke is clearly sympathetic to the former chair, whereas Fairgogh appears to favour Oyl Wynn.

There are key points of divergence between the official and unofficial stories in this scenario. While Wright's story reports objective and verifiable statistics, and is therefore very accurate, it is not necessarily the most powerful or useful story told. The other stories give clues to the tellers' motives, feelings and strategic ways of communicating. In one sense, these unofficial stories bring out a different kind of truth—one that complements rather than conflicts with the factuality of the official story. Just as some truths can be calculated or counted, others will surface more naturally through careful and qualitative interpretation.

The simultaneous presence of these stories at Utopian Products suggests that individual employees will be influenced by the version they hear. Some will welcome the change in leadership, others will view it with caution or even mistrust. The particular version they receive will have a powerful effect on their attitude to management and on their loyalty and devotion to the company's mission and goals. In turn, the employees of Utopian Products will react and contribute to their work in differing ways as a result of the stories they hear about important people and events in the organisation.

Finally, the Utopian Products example suggests one more important thing about many human stories: they can contain 'invented' information. Sometimes people make up stories simply to 'liven up' a dull tale. Slight embellishments, twists and interpretations can make a story entertaining. For example, boastful claims occasionally accompany facts. More often than not, however, the boastful claims are what the story-teller would have *liked* to have said rather than what they really did say. Do these sound familiar?

Boastful claim	Actual events
Boy, did I give it to the boss!	I asked the boss if she would welcome another suggestion.
You'd think World War III broke out when I had it out with him.	I indicated my concern in a discussion with the boss.
I called the manager's bluff.	I decided to pull my socks up.
I told the guy he was off his rocker.	I cautiously asked the boss if he was sure of his business plan.

Lies: the 'shadow side'

Another reason for inventing stories is to make people believe lies or deceitful information. In the workplace, these fabrications are part of the covert culture of organisations. This is the organisational 'shadow side', where communication is typically unpredictable. Gerard Egan, an internationally acclaimed organisational development consultant and scholar, suggests that the shadow side of organisational life is characterised by 'politics of self-interest', while the overt culture of organisations is governed by 'politics of institutional enhancement'.[5] People who engage in the politics of self-interest are often empire-builders. By not communicating their stories openly, however, they do little to prevent the eventual and inevitable downfall of their empires. In essence, the politics of self-interest militates against the prospect of a team culture in the system. When employees begin to realise that their managers are not being open or honest with them, they will counter by creating a 'shadow side' of their own. The manager's empire will thus be divided by an attitude of 'us versus them'.

One of the problems with 'shadow side communication' is that it is virtually impossible to expose a lie without confronting the person about whom the lie is being told. It's hard for us to imagine going to a work colleague and saying 'Are you really sleeping with the head of human resources?' or 'Is it true that your partner has AIDS?'. The best we can hope to do is make intelligent and calculated guesses about the honesty of the story-teller.

In making these guesses, we usually take into account our previous dealings with the story-teller. Were the stories of the past believable? Has there been any corroboration of those stories by subsequent events? When guessing about the truthfulness of a story, we also tend to ask ourselves questions about the reputability and credibility of the story-teller. If we are hearing the story in person, our judgment is probably also influenced by the presenter's non-verbal behaviours—like head nods and gestures, facial expressions and voice qualities.

Of course, we may additionally have formed an impression of the character of the person about whom the story is being told. If the story-teller's words are not consistent with our previous opinion of the 'victim', we may then choose to reject the message with which we are being enjoined to agree or the argument we are being asked to support.

How are people influenced by stories?

Regardless of the different kinds of stories we hear and tell in our daily lives, we tend to look for the gist or 'punchline' of the story. The gist of the story is its main point. When people ask 'What's the movie about?' they want a very concise idea of the plot or storyline:

Telling stories in everyday life

> *Dead Poets' Society*? It's about an inspiring English literature teacher who loses his job because his teaching approaches are too radical.
>
> James Hilton's book, *The Lost Horizon*, is the story of an adventurous Englishman who discovers and eventually settles in Shangri-La, a piece of paradise in Tibet.

Knowing the gist of a story enables us to make certain decisions. Our first decision may be to determine whether we need to know the complete details of the story. We need to decide if the story is worth remembering or not. If we believe it is, our natural tendency is then to decide on whether we agree with or accept the people and actions described in the story. This defines our position on any issue or point of morality in the script. Having worked out our position, our final decision concerns how we should communicate and behave towards the story's 'characters'.

This sequence of decisions represents the process of how people are influenced by stories. It is also a model of human communication, since all that we say and do to others is largely based on our images or impressions of individuals and of our relationships with them. Stories contain these kinds of images, which then become our scripts for living and communicating. In one sense, we can say that *stories provide us with a basis for making strategic choices about our actions and communication with others*.

Keys to persuasion

Any question about how stories can influence people inevitably touches on the area of persuasion. Over the past 50 years, much research has been undertaken on persuasion. Key elements of effective persuasion include the credibility of the story-teller, the use of powerful or emotive language, a skilful and appropriate use of humour and a logical and reasoned argument. It is also vital that the story-teller keeps the interest and attention of the audience, and that the story doesn't become irrelevant.

The credible source

There is general agreement that people are persuaded to believe and accept stories emanating from a highly credible source. The most common dimensions of high credibility are competence (also sometimes referred to as expertise) and trustworthiness (also labelled elsewhere as safety). Some of the more recent scholarship on dimensions of persuasion also identifies dynamism and charisma as important determinants of high credibility. Persuasion theorists argue that if the story-teller is competent, trustworthy and dynamic, the attitudes of audience members are likely to be favourable to the story. The ultimate aim of persuasive stories is attitude change in the listener.

Emotive language
Highly credible story-tellers use a variety of persuasive appeals to help audiences develop positive attitudes to their messages. One commmon persuasive device is the appeal to fear. Most of us can think of fearful messages about the dangers of smoking, drink driving and unsafe sex. Some of these messages have been made into TV community service announcements—like the 'Grim Reaper' advertisement about AIDS and HIV infection. The aim of these appeals is to deter people from doing something which can have tragic consequences.

Fear appeals are really a subset of persuasive appeals based on emotive language. Attitudes to stories can be strongly influenced by emotive words and phrases:

- The customer service here is like an out-of-order antiquated elevator in an unsafe 40-floor building ready for demolition.
- Rather than booming like a well-tuned kettle drum, production is like the hissing of a bow on a cheap violin without strings.
- The team working on this project has as much initiative as a flock of stupid sheep leaping through the gate in pursuit of the creature in front.

Emotive language is usually strengthened by the introduction of derogatory adjectives like 'cheap' or 'tawdry'.

Appropriate humour
Skilled story-tellers also use appropriate humour to persuade their audiences. Jokes, limericks, puns and witty quotations can be powerful devices for adding credibility to the story-teller's image. The stereotypical salesperson is

renowned for having a huge repertoire of amusing anecdotes and stories judiciously used to persuade customers to buy. Mostly, these stories are terse and to the point—the sales message needs tight packaging to make a direct mark on the customer. Often, these stories commence with predictable words like 'Have you heard the one about the chap who . . . ?' or 'How many managers does it take to . . . ?'. These stories are as short as two sentences and, when told with panache, can be catalysts for persuading customers to purchase the product or service in question.

Sometimes humour can be captured in a single sentence or in a company name (which is a bit like a story title), for example, the name of the clothing store for pregnant women 'From Here to Maternity'. Another store, selling mobile telephones is called 'Hold the Phone!'. One ingenious company name for a hair treatment clinic: 'Happy Days are Hair Again'. A creative play on words used in advertising was 'Any baker who kneads the dough is in the Yellow Pages'. Perhaps the most humorously inventive example is the motto of a private investigation and security agency: 'We are De-Buggers You're Looking For'.

There are times when humour is used unintentionally. For example, a student sitting his final high school English literature examination had this to say:

> *The famous English poet John Milton got married and wrote* Paradise Lost. *After his wife died he wrote* Paradise Regained.

Laurence Peter cites this piece of apparently unintentional humour from the *Kansas Bulletin*:

> *Our paper carried the notice last week that Mr Hamilton Ferris is a defective in the police force. This was a typographical error. Mr Ferris is a detective in the police farce.*[6]

A similar example in another paper referred to a veteran war hero as a 'battle-scared general'. When the person in question complained to the paper's editor, an apology appeared in the following day's edition with the added words 'The notice should have read "a bottle-scarred general"'. And another gem was produced by the disc jockey who, in a live interview with the jazz pianist and composer Dave Brubeck, asked how many people there were in his quartet.

These examples suggest that unintentional humour resulting from careless communication can be persuasive in ways story-tellers had not originally intended.

Some jokes are deliberately packaged as stories. For example, there are the 'good news and bad news' jokes we are all familiar with:

> A man develops gangrene in one leg and is told by a surgeon that the leg must be amputated. After the operation, the surgeon visits the patient and says 'I have good news and bad news. Which do you want to hear first?'
> 'Let's have the bad news first,' says the patient.
> 'Well,' says the doctor, 'Unfortunately we sawed off the wrong leg.' When the patient finishes spluttering and gasping with disbelief and shock, he asks 'And what's the good news?'.
> 'You'll love this,' says the surgeon, 'The other leg is getting better.'

Of the various techniques to persuade, humorous story-telling is probably the most risky. Inevitably, there are still some people who will tell unsuitable jokes to their audiences. This happens when story-tellers fail to get to know their listeners and instead assume that everyone they communicate with will react favourably to their stories. Regardless of the sensibilities, gender or ethnicity of their listeners, they blithely recount stories with sexist or racist punchlines. Sometimes the same stories exist in different countries, the object of ridicule generally changing with the location. Many of the Irish stories told in Australia are exactly the same as Polish stories heard in American cities like Chicago. The theme of inappropriate humour will reappear in a later chapter, where strategies for training people to be skilful story-tellers are considered.

Logic and reason
A fourth way to persuade people through story-telling is to use logic or reasoned argument. Logical appeals tend to work better in some situations than others. In a court of law, for example, barristers rely on reliable arguments and evidence to prove their cases. Industrial disputes are often, though not always, settled through reasoned debate. On the other hand, in some settings,

the power of logic is as good as lost. When the weight of evidence, for instance, is of a highly technical kind, some people may simply not understand what is being said. In these circumsances, how persuasively a point is being put hardly matters if the substance of the message is not being received.

Relevance
We would do well to remind ourselves, too, that people will not be persuaded by our stories if they are about things which are not interesting or relevant to our audience. This is often true of managers who think in terms of product- or service-specific ideas. A potentially useful story from a customer service department in a manufacturing firm may not be seen to be relevant to a customer service team in a financial institution. In reality, stories can have very wide applications. Unfortunately, managers who are convinced that their organisations are unique will continue to shape their vision by looking inwards rather than by seizing opportunities to learn from the world outside.

Summary

As we can now appreciate, there are different ways in which people can be influenced by the stories they hear. No single technique is necessarily more potent than any other.

How much individuals will be influenced depends on a number of interdependent factors:

- What is the story about? Is the story topic important or interesting to the listener? Could the story be offensive to certain audiences?
- How believable is the story? Can the story be checked out? Which version of the story is the true one? How can the listener know?
- Where did the story originate? Is the current version first- or second-hand?
- Who is telling the story? Is the story-teller an expert on the topic? Is the story-teller sincere, genuinely believing in the point of the story? How dynamic and charismatic is the story-teller's presentation?
- Why is the story being told? What is the story-teller's motive or aim? Is the story 'old hat?' Is the story-teller 'flogging a dead horse'?

> - Where is the story being told? Is the story related in official or formal settings like committee or board rooms? Or do people hear the story informally via the organisation's grapevine or though socialising in recreation areas like games rooms, gymnasiums, lounges, cafes or bars?
> - What are the consequences, for the listener, of accepting the story? What professional or personal relationships could be affected by such acceptance? What career opportunities could be jeopardised?
> - What damage could the listener cause by recounting the story to someone else?

These factors are useful guidelines for training in communication through story-telling. We will come back to them when we give specific attention to training and development approaches in Chapter 6.

So far we have discovered that story-telling is a fact of life. By learning about stories and the story-telling process we can gain deeper understandings of our communication and personal and professional relationships with other people in our life. We have seen that people tell stories for reasons ranging from tension release to changing the attitudes of their listeners. Additionally, we have noted that although stories may be formally scripted or informal, they all have the potential to influence our thinking, communication and behaviour.

2

the story-telling organisation

Too bad that all the people who know how to run the country are busy driving taxi cabs and cutting hair...
George Burns

Now that we've seen how stories are part of our everyday lives, let us turn to the workplace. How can our organisations be seen as places where stories are told? Why are stories told in organisations and who tells these stories? Some of the different kinds of stories communicated by people in human systems will be reviewed as will the skills people need to tell and listen to stories in their own organisations.

What is a story-telling organisation?

An organisation can be likened to a human body. The members constitute the various parts of that body. David Boje went a step further, coining the term 'the story-telling organisation'—he saw stories as 'the blood vessels through which changes pulsate in the heart of organisational life'.[1] As the blood is pumped by the heart though the organisational body, the member parts are renewed and revitalised. Members' zest for quality work and productivity are enhanced when they are energised through their blood supply. Just as stories are an organisation's blood vessels, 'communication is the lifeblood of systems'.[2] Organisations whose stories have characters and plots that enlighten and enrich their members through frequent communication are the healthiest story-telling systems. People in such organisations are likely to want to become an established part of the story-telling culture.

All the parts of an efficiently operating body work interdependently. If one part of the body is ailing or malfunctioning, the rest of the working parts are likely to be affected. The story-telling organisation is no exception to this analogy.

Without system-wide stories, each part of the organisation becomes a sub-system with its own set of stories and culture. The body does not function as an integrated whole but rather as a set of discrete organs, muscles, tissues and nerves. Instead of helping other parts of the body to work as well as possible, the independent subsystems become concerned only with their own well-being and survival. As a result, the body eventually suffers entropy—the tendency for a system to become disordered and thus to self-destruct gradually.

In the story-telling organisation, there is collective creation, telling, maintenance and revision of what is known and understood by its parts. Story-telling is a continual process. Each story-teller creates a small piece of a larger jigsaw puzzle. When all the stories are told, shared and interpreted, the pieces can be fitted together to form an overall picture. No individual in an organisation knows the whole story, but by listening to the stories of other members, that person can understand an event or human action from a broader perspective. In an unhealthy story-telling organisation, not all possible stories are told or heard.

By contrast, the healthy story-telling organisation affords opportunities for all stakeholders, including customers and clients, to be heard. Just as the brain sends life-preserving messages via neural impulses to different parts of the body, or as the heart ensures the circulation of blood throughout the system, so stories in the healthy story-telling organisation give life to the energies of people in different geographic and strategic locations.

Why do people in organisations tell stories?

Now that we have an idea of what the story-telling organisation is like, let's consider why people in organisations tell stories. In the previous chapter, this question was asked in the broader context of stories in everyday life. Although working in organisations is part of everyday living, we will concentrate on people's reasons and motives for telling stories in professional work settings.

There are several reasons for people to be story-tellers in their workplaces. Some of these reasons have been alluded to already, but these reasons deserve a closer examination.

Enhancing learning and creating meaning

The main purpose of story-telling in organisations is to convert information and facts into stories that help members make sense of their organisation and which can inspire them to greater achievements and productivity. In making sense of their organisations, people go through formative and powerful learning experiences. So, an important aim of the story-telling organisation is to promote learning. Charles Vance describes story-telling as '... a valuable tool in the management of learning in organisations'.[3]

The kind of learning that can take place through organisational story-telling is not only about company policies and practices—but also about the emotions that people have in their professional lives. It has been argued that '... story-telling is a fundamental force shaping the emotional climate of the organisation'.[4]

Because there is a close connection between story-telling and learning, we could say that the story-telling organisation complements the 'learning organisation'.[5] Learning and story-telling are like the yin and yang of organisational life. We learn through the story-telling of others and by telling stories we help others to learn. The umbrella under which story-telling and learning are linked is *communication*. Story-telling is a special kind of communication. It is the process in which two or more persons share, examine, interpret or challenge common past experiences and probable future experiences. Like all human communication, story-telling involves creating meanings from our experiences. These meanings, in turn, become our guidelines for behaviour and relating to others.

Staying informed

Another analogy for the story-telling organisation is a mansion with many rooms, where people do a lot of talking as part of their work. As long as people in one room know what stories are being told in another room, the upkeep of the mansion will continue to be smooth and efficient. What happens in one room could affect the entire household. Imagine the uproar in parts of the house when someone who is doing electrical repairs in one room turns off the electricity for the whole house without first notifying the other rooms' occupants.

People who work together can avoid problems of this kind by sharing 'stories'. In this way, members of the story-telling organisation keep each other informed at all times. It is important, therefore, for individuals to have access to other members of the organisation. The best kind of contact for story-listening and learning is face-to-face contact. When people communicate in person, they do not only listen to words but can also observe important non-verbal cues which accompany the words. In the case of stories aimed at attitude change in the listener, the non-verbal cues of the story-teller can be very persuasive.

Of course, there are other ways modern technology enables us to keep in contact with others. A smorgasbord of electronic media—mobile telephones, fax machines, electronic mail and computer links across streets, suburbs and the world—help us to know what's going on even if certain individuals are not always accessible. Most modern organisations have these facilities available for the networking of staff and other important stakeholders like clients and external consultants.

Facilitating change

Another important reason for story-telling is to facilitate strategic changes and developments in organisations. If people move from room to room in their story-telling mansion and have conversations and share stories wherever they may be, the organisation will be dynamic rather than static. In the healthy story-telling organisation the only constant is change. By the same token, the collective wisdom of story-tellers will ensure that change is not expected simply for change's sake.

How stories can expedite change in systems

Mr Brad Awl, the chief executive officer (CEO) of the Laurel Industrial Toolmaking Company, was becoming increasingly concerned about stories of theft and pilfering on the factory site. He wanted to change the attitudes and actions of certain employees, who were suspected but could not be identified for certain.

Calling a meeting of production supervisors, Brad explained the problem and urged the supervisory team to think of incentives to lure employees away from thieving. In a brainstorming meeting, these managers came up with the idea of regular staff competitions, where the winners would be rewarded with selected products of the company. The competitions would be for individual staff members to suggest new ways of extending career opportunities for staff development and advancement. Previous winners would be rostered to join panels to judge future competitions but would otherwise be eligible to enter more competitions.

The scheme was tried out over a 12 month period. During this time, not only did the thieving cease totally, but the morale of staff also increased correspondingly. By the end of the year, many individuals volunteered ideas for new competitions via the suggestion box in the staff recreation area.

What stories in this sequence of events were told to help along the changes which eventually came about? Brad Awl gave his management team a brief story about the need to find ways of encouraging employees to give up stealing. Next, the supervisors collectively created a new story about competitive challenges for staff. With each new competition, individuals freely chose to devise stories about how the company could be improved. When the scheme was in place, judges on the competition panels constructed stories about prize winners. The company became a healthy story-telling organisation because the stories that were valued were aimed at making the organisation a pleasant and rewarding place.

Part I: Communicating through stories

Mapping the big picture

Stories become learning tools when people begin to see their organisation from as many story-tellers' viewpoints as possible. Organisational development consultants need this kind of 'whole picture' before recommending specific strategic initiatives to energise the establishment. Let's take the example of Zappy Electrical Appliance Discounts. Sales have fallen by 30 per cent during the past 12 months. Why has this been happening? Here are five separate accounts:

Story A
Ms Flora Walker, Manager of the Kitchenware Electrical Appliances Department, says that customers are no longer duped by marketing gimmicks like 'free bonus offers' with every purchase. They would rather pay less for the item they actually need.

Story B
Mr Gus Tommah, who is shopping for a bargain price pop-up toaster, says that discount shops are no longer any cheaper than major department stores. You can get the same item with better warranties at a department store prepared to match any price.

Story C
Mr Alec Trishan, a retired repairer and tradesperson, claims that 'they don't make things like they used to'. It's not worth repairing appliances nowadays because the cost of repairs to today's models is about as much as buying new goods. So people are hanging on to older appliances that still work rather than buying newer, low-quality items.

Story D
For several minutes, Ms R. U. Free has been vainly looking for someone to serve her. She is appalled at the decline of customer service in modern shops and stores, especially in discount houses.

Story E
Mr T. Najer, a university student who was interviewed by a market survey consultant at the front door of Zappy Discounts, said he didn't need appliances because he didn't eat home-cooked food much. You could live quite comfortably by having meals at cheap fast food restaurants.

It's evident from these different stories that there are at least five possible reasons for the fall in sales at Zappy Electrical Appliance Discounts. Those who look for the whole picture are more likely to find comprehensive solutions to organisational problems because they see the problem from many angles. Each angle may suggest, as it did in this example, a different reason for the problem. Thus, by addressing problems from multiple perspectives, organisations can be mapped with greater accuracy.

Satisfying individual needs

People in organisations often tell stories for personal reasons, including the achievement of personal goals or ambitions. For example, if particular individuals have had problems in relating to others in the organisation, they could generate stories to cause trouble to their perceived adversaries. Think of two candidates for a vacant promotional position in an organisation. The competition could be healthy—or it could become spiteful. When ambition overrides collegiality either candidate could resort to telling stories which smear the reputation and credibility of their opponent. Tactics of this kind have a twofold purpose: first, to reduce the other's chances of promotion and, second, to put oneself in a good light.

We can all probably think of instances when someone made up a story about a person to gain some advantage over them, discrediting one achievement by finding a corresponding flaw in another aspect of professional work. At one university, several lecturers denigrated colleagues who committed themselves to time-consuming research projects in addition to their expected teaching allocations. The reason for criticising those undertaking research as well as teaching was that the quality of teaching was presumed to suffer. It was believed, therefore, that research in some way interfered with teaching.

In reality, the criticism was unfounded, since the best teachers, especially at postgraduate levels, were generally the most informed and up-to-date experts in their field. That expertise could only come from dedicated scholarship.

In the story-telling organisation, people may tell stories for other personal reasons—like letting off steam, defending themselves against an attack by someone else, or showing that they are involved in the life of the system.

Part I: Communicating through stories

We are all familiar with the need to release tension on occasions. 'Sounding off' to a close friend is a common practice for most people when they feel under attack or unjustly treated, when they want to vindicate their own position and cast aspersions on the motives and actions of an aggressor.

When people want to show their involvement in organisational life, they tell stories with a subtext that says 'Hey, please notice me. Isn't what I'm doing worth a few Brownie points?'. People usually resort to attention-seeking if their efforts or accomplishments at work continue to go unnoticed. Very healthy story-telling organisations probably have few individuals who exhibit attention-seeking behaviour, since everyone's stories are likely to be heard and shared. Story-telling organisations, therefore, encourage open communication and thus minimise the incidence of individual members needing to publicise their achievements.

Sometimes people who have been unexceptional in the performance of their duties tell stories that tend to elevate mediocrity to excellence. When this happens, it becomes difficult for managers to appraise the story-teller's performance as anything less than very good, without appearing to be destructive or oblivious to the apparently conscientious efforts of those they are supervising. The converse effect of putting oneself in a good light is to create the impression that others whose actions differ from the story-teller's are less worthy organisational members.

Whether the stories of organisational members are based on truth or not, collectively they provide a gauge for determining a system's culture. When communication is open, stories can help people to create shared meanings through systematic and structured reflections of shared experiences. For instance, people will talk about former CEOs. In doing so, they will look back on significant events and times during the CEO's term of office. Shared positive feelings and recollections can reinforce positive feelings about the organisation. On the other hand, unpleasant memories may predispose story-tellers to paint less favourable pictures of the organisation in their stories.

What are organisational stories about?

Organisational stories are about lives and experiences of people in an organisation. Stories are the tools by which organisational members communicate—

they are like measuring instruments that indicate the state of the organisation's health. A feel for an organisation's culture can be picked up from the stories going around. From organisational stories, we can learn something about the level of satisfaction felt by the system's members, the quality of life in the organisation, the quality and kinds of personal and professional relationships and whether the organisation has 'get up and go'.

In any compendium of an organisation's stories, we would also learn about people's triumphs and defeats, comic and tragic times, loves won and loves lost, and occasions remembered as happy or sad. Through stories, we would learn about the kinds of games people play—psychological, sexual and political. It would not take very long for someone who has heard all these stories to realise what is and what is not valued in the organisation. In this way, we can gauge the organisation's tolerance of us as individuals and of what we stand for.

Many organisational stories are chronicled in official documents like annual reports, policy statements and board meeting minutes. These give us one side of the organisation's culture—the formal, official side. Much of the history of the organisation and of how the thinking of members has evolved over time is contained in these types of official papers. Other written formalised stories may be found in in-house newsletters and magazines, bulletins from industrial unions and notices on noticeboards. While there may be more than one story on a particular subject or topic, different versions need not agree as they may be constructed from very specific stakeholder perspectives. Thus, in the case of possible industrial action such as a strike, the union leaders may justify the proposed action on the grounds of protest against discriminatory work practices, whereas the management may see this as an impossible claim but one with a potentially realistic fallback position. Alternatively, customers affected by the strike action may attribute the strike to the excessive demands of power- and money-hungry left-wing employees.

In Chapter 4, heroes and legendary characters who feature prominently in many organisational myths will be examined more closely. At this point, however, it is important to note that some stories in the story-telling organisation live on for many years and become remembered as myths or legends. Traditionally, myths have been classified as stories about gods, and legends as stories about heroes. Often, organisational myths have focused on themes like how the organisation was created or how the organisation was saved at some time of crisis by some revered pioneer.

For the most part, however, organisational stories are about the daily lives of the organisation's members. They need not be stories which endure. Most day-to-day stories are told only as long as the subject or issue has sustainable currency and interest. We can readily think of these kinds of topics. Do these kinds of statements and questions sound familiar?

- Why isn't Mary at work today? What's the story?
- Do you want to hear about the movie we saw last night?
- The skiing was great over the weekend at Thredbo. You've got to hear this to believe it about the snow cover on the slopes.
- Have you heard that Bill has left his wife and is now living with his secretary? I can give you the low-down on this one.

These kinds of stories may only be told once or twice to good friends at work or to amiable professional acquaintances. People tell stories like these to pass the time of day or to take time out from their work to converse socially. When the stories have importance, relevance, interest or appeal to a larger audience, they tend to be retold more often. Sometimes, alarming stories such as the ones below can trigger an escalating story-telling sequence.

- Is it true that our company branch has to downsize by 20 staff? The story I heard is that . . .
- The price of company shares has fallen by $2. Do you know what this means for us, the employees?
- Here's how the company restructuring will work. There'll be fewer chiefs and more Indians. I guess some of us will get demoted.
- We've lost so much business recently we're going to have to close down our rural branches.

The managerial parable

When there are status, power or positional differences between the story-teller and the story-listener(s), the stories can take on a didactic, moralistic tone or flavour. This can happen when the story-teller is the superior addressing an employee. The story can become a managerial parable. Parables are short allegorical stories containing some basic truth or moral lesson. Managerial parables have been used to bring insubordinate staff into line. As such, managerial parables can have a threatening quality about them.

> Mr J. Olwarder: Ah, Lowan, come in and take a seat. Looks like we need to sort out a few things, eh?
> Mr Lowan Wolfe: Don't know what you mean, J.O. What am I supposed to have done?
> Mr Olwarder: You don't seem to want to be a team player. Do you know how many people's feathers you've ruffled lately?
> Mr Wolfe: Aren't you making too much of a few differences of opinion I've had with one or two people? It's no big deal, J.O.
> Mr Olwarder: Son, let me tell you a little story about an administrator we once had who wanted to be a one-person band. This guy would be placed in a team, then do by himself all the work the team was supposed to do. Once he'd finished the job, he'd give it to his manager with the added message that he'd got no help from his team mates. The manager eventually decided there was no need for teams to do the work of the administrator, who could handle every routine job that came along. The former team members were assigned to new teams that did not require them to work with the administrator. Pretty soon the administrator began to feel he was being exploited—he believed he was doing much more than anyone else. The quality of his work suffered and his manager gave him a formal warning to pick up his act. Meanwhile, those working in teams became very productive and were praised for their efficiency and high-level performance. Does this story remind you of anyone you know?

Managerial parables may sound patronising. They are sometimes applied indiscriminately and directed to staff who are genuinely doing a good job. When managers use parables to discipline staff, they run the risk of being perceived as parents treating those reporting to them as children.

Who are the story-tellers in organisations?

Since story-telling is one way of managing communication in organisations, there is a natural tendency for some to assume that the story-tellers are the senior managers—the change agents with most power to control interpersonal communication and the system's culture. But just as every member of an organisation, regardless of their status or position, has a communication management role to play,[6] all people in systems are potential story-tellers.

Not all story-tellers work in the same way. Some people, for example, have a talent for creating stories. They observe what is happening around them and then package their perceptions into a tellable tale. These are the originators of long-lasting stories and their visions can have a powerful impact on change within their organisations.

Other organisational members are good at recounting the stories generated by someone else. Their skill is in polishing the presentation and giving it vitality, while at the same time preserving the story's factual integrity and accuracy. Among this group are the 'history-tellers'. Their stories are intended to be remembered by future generations of workers and employees. Because they care about preserving the best aspects of the organisation's current and past culture, they treat their stories as slices of life and history. If any change is to come as a result of history-telling, it is because the lessons of the past are seized upon as pointers for today's organisation members. We can all learn how to repeat successes, just as we can all be on our guard to avoid repeating mistakes.

In the story-telling organisation, many of the participants have the skill to listen to the stories of others and then to interpret them. The interpretation can involve teasing out the 'moral' or 'lesson' of the story.

When an organisation's members look for the lesson in a story, they ask themselves questions like:

- What is the story-teller's motive?
- What communication or action does the story-teller expect of the story-listener?
- Who will tell the story next?
- Who will hear the story next?
- How will the organisation's culture be affected by this story?
- Does this story suggest new policy directions for the organisation?
- Can we extract a 'proverb' from the story?

We are all familiar with proverbs like 'a stitch in time saves nine' or 'a rolling stone gathers no moss'. There are, in addition, popular wise sayings which could become the moral or lesson for many managerial stories and actions:

- While managers do things right, leaders do the right things.[7]
- Successful managers 'manage by walking around' (MBWA) rather than by 'kicking staff in the ass'(KITA).[8]
- Good managers are prepared to take calculated risks.
- Chieftains should avoid doing battle when both winning and losing will cost too much.[9]

Sometimes, wise thoughts are found in provocative questions like:

- If the basic mission of the organisation is teaching, why are the salaries of administrators higher than the salaries of teachers?
- Why do bureaucrats frustrate workers by constantly generating complex and unnecessary new forms to be completed?
- While administrative responsibilities are being devolved down the line, why is there no corresponding devolution of additional funds or staff?

Regardless of whether organisational members create, recreate or interpret stories, they are part of a story-telling network. As we have seen, people use stories in different ways. Through stories people experience organisational life, adapt to it, and, if necessary, learn how to survive it.

How are stories communicated?

From the moment people arrive at work to the time they leave it, they find communicating with others inevitable. The first person they speak to may be a window cleaner or an elevator operator. When they get a cup of coffee, they may hold a brief conversation with others. Before entering their offices, they are likely to greet a number of colleagues from various sections of their organisation, including their own.

Part I: Communicating through stories

In the course of the working day, different groups of people form to deal with shared professional matters and personal concerns. When meetings are concluded, individuals go to their telephones, their computerised workstations or to other people's offices and communicate afresh with yet another person. At the end of the working day, some members may relax over a quiet drink and chat before going home. Although there are undoubtedly times during the day when people work by themselves, it is hard to imagine any organisation where some kind of interpersonal contact, no matter how small, does not occur for every member.

In all these different types of communication between people at work, a lot of stories are heard and told. Story-telling is the process by which people communicate in their organisations. Through story-telling, people construct images about themselves and their relationships to others. These images become personal guidelines for relating to colleagues and important stakeholders like clients and consultants. With more and more experience of these people, images can be fine-tuned and reshaped if necessary. Our images, therefore, are like prompts to tell our stories, or explanatory internal databases to help us interpret the stories of others.

Since communication is really about meaning-making through the creation of images, story-tellers need to understand that the images they construct become the meanings that determine their actions towards others. The ability to create meanings is not confined to senior managers, although high level executives certainly cannot do without this essential attribute. Warren Bennis said that the management of meaning is one of five key competencies of successful leaders. In particular, Bennis was suggesting that meaning management involves helping staff understand the leader's dreams and visions.[10] The communicative art of story-telling is thus an aspect of organisational leadership. Just how well a person's leadership is accepted by staff will be reflected in the degree to which those staff members understand and are able to restate the vision and dream told in the leader's story.

Stories told face-to-face

Not everyone in an organisation, however, is a visionary. Most people create meanings about the people, relationships and happenings that are important to them personally and professionally. It is natural for all of us to form impressions about people with whom we are on good terms as well as about people with whom we do not get along. Equally natural is our desire to communicate these impressions to others, who we hope will sympathise with us. The best way we can let others know how we feel about someone is to tell a story about that person. These stories are generally about something which has already happened to someone. Some stories, however, are about hypothetical future events or scenarios. They can be about plans, goals or strategies, for instance. In such cases, the opening line typically invites a response from the listener:

- I'd like your reaction to the proposal I'm going to run past you.
- Tell me if you think my strategy, which I'll outline for you now, is likely to work.
- After this presentation, your views on the suitability of these production targets would be helpful.
- Here's my thinking about how we should handle the situation. Perhaps you may come up with a better approach once you've heard what I've got in mind.

Sometimes, the audience reactions we look for are supportive value judgments. Often the opening line of our stories in these instances betray our own values and our wish to have these supported by our listeners. Emotive words can also intensify the slant of our stories, as the following examples show:

- If you were me would you believe that snake who tried to put one over me last time? This is the excuse that the scheming wimp wants me to accept.
- Am I right in questioning the sincerity of someone whom everyone regards as a compulsive liar? The fraud would have me believe that . . .
- How could I put that lazy so-and-so in charge? Should I take the risk when the agenda specifications are . . . ?

Stories in writing

Story-telling can also occur through written correspondence. When we receive stories in writing, we tend to agree or disagree with the story-teller more definitely than we would if we hear the story-teller's 'live' version. Many people think there is something very final about the printed word, as though the story has been thought through carefully over several oral versions before it has been eventually committed to paper. If the story's teller has signed the written document, the 'finality' of the version is underscored even more. It cannot be disclaimed by the story-teller—unless the signature is a fake. There is a kind of legal aura about printed messages. As long as spoken stories are not recorded in any way (on video or audio tape, for example) they reside in the minds of story-tellers and story-listeners. Written or printed stories, however, are unchanging records that can be repeatedly consulted.

Because of this, good managers only commit to writing stories that can be readily authenticated or substantiated. However, spoken versions can be distorted in the retelling process and the originators of stories may find it easier to disown certain facts or details. In a sense, it may be true that while stories in writing tend to be formal and therefore part of the open culture of organisations, spoken stories are often punctuated by informal thinking more frequently associated with the organisational 'shadow side'.

Naturally, much will depend on how and when the story is made known. A public announcement at a company's annual general meeting is no less formal than the same message on a written circular. A privately shared written note destroyed on receipt is as much a part of the covert culture of an organisation as a whispered piece of gossip.

Singing in the wires

Two other contemporary media via which organisational stories can be shared are telephones and computers. The telephone message is vocal, live but not face-to-face. Body information like facial expressions, head movements, postures and gestures is not available to us. Non-verbal cues from the face and body can often tell us something about the story-teller's credibility.

Computers allow us to exchange printed messages through electronic mail. Stories contained in these messages can be saved and permanently stored on computer disk files. The advantage of electronic mail over ordinary internal mail is that it is generally very quick. Electronically communicated stories can be acted on without any delay. Of course, they can also be passed on to others to read but when this happens meaning-making may be more difficult as the context becomes further removed.

These processes are now an inevitable part of the daily life of people in human systems. Through the stories told and received in these different ways members of the organisation learn from each other what is expected of them, what needs to be done, and what skills they need to develop in order to be successful.

Story-telling skills

Individuals can impress us with their ability to entertain us with a story. Sometimes, these are public figures—eloquent speechmakers who stir our imaginations and emotions. Many after-dinner speakers are chosen to speak at conferences or on other special occasions because they can tell a story well. Among our own circle of friends, we can probably think of at least one person who is a gifted raconteur. And we have all known individuals who are superb at telling jokes. What makes these people good at story-telling and how are they different from less persuasive, inventive or amusing story-tellers?

Meaning-making

Skilled story-tellers have developed communication competence. In part, this means that they understand that human communication is a process of meaning-making and that the role of a good story-teller is to help listeners construct meanings about the story they are experiencing. Good story-tellers do this by structuring their stories in such a way that the language and concepts used are familiar and appropriate to the target audience.

Unfortunately, even as children many people are exposed to unintelligible information. We have all heard children say at times that they were unable to understand their teachers at school. For instance, it would be pointless to ask schoolchildren to write stories about places they had never been to, or creatures they had never seen, with any understanding. A teacher in an inner-city primary school asked the pupils to write stories about their favourite farmyard animals. Not one child had ever been out of the city.

Using analogies, comparisons and metaphors

Skilled story-tellers avoid allusions to the unfamiliar and build instead on things which are known and understood by their listeners. Story-readers or

Part I: Communicating through stories

listeners, however, should be fed a diet of more than merely familiar or known concepts. If people receive known concepts only, they never learn anything new.

One clue to successful story-telling is to start from the known and understood and gradually move to the new material. In doing this, skilled story-tellers will make sure that each new idea is explained or described carefully to enable the receiver to construct a meaningful image. One useful way of linking new material with old is to use analogies or comparisons, for example:

- Career path planning is like learning the design of an organisational labyrinth where some avenues lead to dead ends while others open doors to new spaces.
- Managerial risk-taking is like checking the depth of a rock pool with a stick before diving in.
- Policy-based changes in organisations are often like having to learn new skills without understanding why those skills are important.

Strategic managers are usually good at planning, problem-solving and decision-making through the application of analogies. This is a form of creative thinking that has been the focus of executive development programs. Participants are typically asked to liken their organisational problem to something else. For example, the organisation's present inefficient structure may be compared to a four-legged table with one leg about to collapse. Alternatively, poor leadership in an organisation may be compared to an orchestra playing a symphony without a conductor.

In one workshop, all the participants were asked to think of a metaphor for their organisation. They were asked to complete the sentence 'My organisation is like . . .'. Their organisation consisted of three departments. Frequent interdepartmental communication was considered by many participants as critical for the organisation's well-being and survival. Some of the metaphors developed by workshop participants carried an implication of what would happen if an organisational component became dysfunctional, as illustrated in their responses given below.

The story-telling organisation

My organisation is like:

- a triceratops (a dinosaur with three horns)—each horn represents a section or department in the organisation)
- a tricycle (each wheel representing a department)—the tricycle would collapse if one of the wheels broke
- The Three Stooges (each Stooge representing a department)—at times all three work well together; at other times they keep hitting and hurting each other
- a crew of three on a sailing boat (each crew member representing a department)—successful sailing depends on the interdependence and co-operation of crew members
- a chamber orchestra consisting of string, woodwind and brass sections (each section representing a department)—the three sections need to harmonise in order to create a symphonic effect
- an infantry company of three platoons (each platoon representing a department)—the company commander is assisted by three platoon leaders
- a three-person mountain climbing team (each person represents a department)—the safety of each climber depends on co-operation between the team members
- three vertically positioned dominoes (each domino represents a department)—if one domino falls onto another, all three will topple over
- a musical three-part invention (each part represents a department)—the three parts collectively form the entire musical opus
- a surgical team in a hospital operating theatre (the surgeon, anaesthetist and theatre nurse represent the departments and the patient is the client or customer)—the interdependence and co-operation of all three is critical for the patient's survival.

All these metaphors were discussed by the participants as the first part of an organisational strategic planning exercise. Each metaphor creator was asked to elaborate on the analogy. The workshop facilitators asked them 'Tell us why you think your organisation is like a . . .'. In effect, the participants were being asked to tell a story around their metaphors.

At least three lessons could be drawn from observation of and participation in this exercise. First of all, some participants found it nearly impossible to think of a metaphor when originally asked, but seemed more able to think freely and come up with metaphors once they had heard other participants' ideas. Initially, then, these people found it hard to generate a story about their organisation. When this happened, they tended to ridicule the workshop exercise, referring to it as a childish game. By contrast, once they did think up a metaphor, their attitude to the exercise appeared to change. It seemed that their enthusiasm for the activity corresponded with their ability to participate in it successfully.

Secondly, it appeared that those who could think up metaphors without help were better strategic thinkers than those who could not. Strategic thinkers need to be able to see 'the big picture'. Metaphors are big picture outlines—the details can be filled in later. The non-strategic thinkers in this exercise were those who wanted to start with details and gradually build up to the big picture. People who think in details or specific terms typically see themselves as 'practical' and unconcerned with esoteric things like metaphors. In progressive organisations, however, the reality is that practicalities only find meaning when they can be located within the big picture or vision of the change facilitators.

The third lesson learned was that initially poor and unimaginative story-tellers could eventually develop into quite competent ones—if they were prepared to learn by observing the more creatively skilled story-tellers. In a sense, the strategic plan workshop afforded a staff development opportunity which some of the more open-minded participants capitalised upon. Those who took this opportunity learned a good deal and became more positive about participating in future workshops. Most importantly, they became better story-tellers.

Involving the audience

Good story-tellers never give away a punch line in the same way inexperienced joke-tellers do. One of the skills of story-telling is to keep the listeners interested, enthralled and glued to their seats, wondering what is going to come next. Alfred Hitchcock, the famous movie director, had a knack of finding stories which held viewers in suspense until the very end. Often these stories had unpredictable twists and climaxes. In *Psycho*, for example, Anthony Perkins played a male psychopathic killer who dressed in women's clothing in order to recreate and act out fantasies of violence while pretending to be someone else. Another Hitchcock classic film was *Spellbound*, in which a doctor suffering from amnesia gradually discovered, with psychiatric help in dream interpretation, the identity of a murderer. Good story-tellers like Hitchcock don't give everything away at once—they keep their audiences guessing about facts that have not yet been revealed.

In some situations, skilled story-tellers know how to get their audiences involved in the story-telling process. An everyday example is the 'shaggy dog story'. Have you ever been in a group where someone began to tell a rather long story that became punctuated with occasional comments from others in the group? Here, the basic story-line is embellished with spontaneously invented facts and details supplied by various individuals in the group. This is a good example of co-story-telling. The effect of co-story-telling is to unite the group. A kind of solidarity develops when everyone has a chance to contribute to the story. As a simple guideline for good story-telling, use this checklist of questions before proceeding:

Checklist for good story-telling

- Is this the right kind of person (or group of people) for me to be telling this story to?
- Do I have a clear reason for wanting to tell this story to this person? Do I believe in my story? Do I like the story I'm telling? Is my attitude to my story likely to 'turn off' my audience?
- Is this the right kind of story or the right version to tell to this audience? Could this story offend or hurt the receiver? Is the story likely to be meaningless to the audience? Is the story in poor taste?
- Is this the right time to be telling this story? Is this the most appropriate place for me to tell this story?
- How can I keep my story-telling as simple and as brief as possible? Is my story longer or more complicated than it need be?
- If I am presenting my story in person rather than in writing, am I aware of the effect of my non-verbal cues on my audience? Non-verbal cues include

Part I: Communicating through stories

- my tone of voice, the volume and rhythm of my speech, how fast I'm talking, the clarity of my enunciation, my facial expressions, gestures and body posture and positioning.
- If I tell my story, how will it affect my long-term personal or professional relationship with the person hearing it?
- Have I got the story straight? Could any of the facts or details be questioned or challenged by the receiver?
- Is the story believable? Are the characters portrayed convincingly by me? Have I been unjust in my description of any person in the story?
- Am I creating a sense of mystery or intrigue? How captivated do my audience members seem to be? Do their non-verbal cues suggest that they are not gripped by my story? Or do they appear to be rapt?
- Am I using the most suitable kind of language and vocabulary? Could I be making a better choice of words? Is there an overkill with slang and colloquial terms? Am I developing colourful and unusual images through the judicious and sensitive use of figurative language (such as metaphors)?
- Am I using the right kinds of persuasive appeals to my audience? Am I showing an appropriate sense of humour? Is my use of emotive language justified? Are fear appeals necessary? Is the story logical? Does it make sense?
- Do my audience members see me, the story-teller, as a 'presence'? How can I tell from the way they react when I tell my story? Is there a respectful hush when I begin? Do they interrupt me as I'm telling my story?
- Should I encourage my audience to interact with me while I tell my story? Would it be appropriate to invite my audience members to be co-producers of the story? Or should I demand silence and attention while I'm telling my story?
- By telling this story, how will I be contributing to the organisation? Will it be better to live in or work if I tell my story? Is my story going to help the organisation towards its strategic goals and mission?

There are other questions, undoubtedly, which we could think of to include in our checklist. You could add to this list by thinking of someone you consider to be a good story-teller. What qualities or considerations could you add to the list above? In some situations, there may be special or context-specific issues. For example, in some organisations male story-tellers may lack credibility when addressing certain women's groups. Similarly, at specific religious or ethnic protest rallies, the motives of politicians whose religious affiliations or ethnic backgrounds do not match those of the group in question may be treated with suspicion and caution.

Story-listening skills

So far we have concentrated on the skills of story-telling. But what about the skills of story-listening? What does it take to be an effective receiver of stories? In many organisations, as part of their staff development, managers undertake interpersonal communication skills training courses. Central to all these courses is the skill of listening. Good, or 'active', listening typically involves the ability to:

- suspend judgment (be non-evaluative)
- reflect feelings ('empathise')
- give accurate feedback.

Each one of these abilities is important for different reasons.

Suspending judgment

If people judge what they are listening to—and this is a very normal tendency—they will not always be able to reproduce with accuracy the story-teller's actual message. Instead, what they can produce is an interpreted version of the story. The interpretations become remembered parts of the story and bits of the original version simply disappear from memory. In some contexts, like courtrooms or parliamentary chambers, judging another's statements and stories is a vital skill and has been legitimately labelled 'critical listening'.[11]

Unfortunately, judgments are often based on stereotypes about the story-teller. These stereotypes can influence our ability to receive information in the way intended by the story-teller and change our perception of the story-teller's credibility. Stereotyping occurs when we assign certain characteristics to particular groups of people. A stereotypical image of lawyers is that they are all obsessed with becoming rich by bleeding their clients dry.

Accountants, similarly, have been stereotyped as dull people interested only in money and with little time for the feelings of those they serve.

Among the most unpleasant and damaging stereotypes are those about people from specific national, religious or ethnic groups. The stereotypes become even more pointed when they also focus on males or females in those groups. For instance, the Australian male has been stereotyped as a beer-drinking, lazy, football fanatic in a blue singlet and shorts. English men have been stereotyped as conservative and reserved in their expression of feelings, Spanish people as hot-blooded and fiery and the Scots as parsimonious. There are stereotypes about American tourists being loud and vulgar, the violent temperaments of Serbs and Croatians, and the self-effacing and hard-working nature of Asians. Examples of religious stereotypes include a presumption of the snobbishness of certain Protestant denominations, the fanaticism of Muslims and the avarice of Jewish people.

Needless to say, this kind of stereotyping can be very damaging to human relationships. In particular, it can affect the way people listen to others, since the speakers are judged before they have told their stories. If people hold a stereotype of a specific group, based on a negative characteristic, for example, they tend to develop a set of connotations or related meanings.

These connotations may be unwarranted and simply not true. Nevertheless, it is natural for people to speculate about others on the basis of stereotypical beliefs or attributed characteristics. Good story-listeners, therefore, should be sensitive to the danger of applying stereotypes to the people with whom they communicate and from whom they hear stories.

Reflecting feelings: empathy

Empathy, the second ability of active listening, is also an important skill for story-listeners, especially when the story is personal and emotionally charged. Active listeners know how to reflect feelings without making gratuitous value judgments. The simplest way to think of the reflective response is that it mirrors an expressed feeling:

> Story-teller: I felt insignificant and humiliated yesterday when the boss dressed me down in front of the other staff members.
> Story-listener: The rebuke the boss gave you yesterday made you feel small.

> Story-teller: I felt completly disoriented and depressed when my executive assistant gave me her notice of resignation yesterday.
> Story-listener: You must have felt awful—like you lost your right arm.

So, reflective responses mirror feelings, either by gentle repetition of the relevant part of the emotional statement or by some paraphrase of it. Sensitive story-listeners who can use reflective responses skilfully actually help and encourage story-tellers to tell their stories right to the end. Empathy is a skill used in a variety of story-telling situations where the story-tellers are giving vent to their feelings by recounting experiences with painful memories. Psychotherapists use this technique to assist their patients to work through and resolve their emotional problems.

Giving accurate feedback

The third skill of active listening is the ability to give accurate feedback to the speaker. Story-tellers will not know if their listeners have got their story straight unless they can hear the story repeated in the way that it was told and intended to be remembered. Poor listening can result in poor performance. Imagine a manager giving a staff member instructions which were not grasped at the time they were issued. Unless that manager has checked on the employee's understanding of the instruction, the task that is undertaken will be based on imperfect interpretations of the manager's directive. Any inadequacy in performance will be compounded if the employee does not speak up and ask the manager for clarification of the task's requirements.

The ability to give accurate feedback depends on the ability to suspend judgment. To be able to repeat or paraphrase a story-teller's message, we must be careful not to impose our own biases or views on what we are hearing. This can be very difficult when the story we are hearing contains beliefs, views, opinions and values which clearly contradict ours. Although we may disagree strongly with the story-teller, our ability to listen will still be evident if we can restate the speaker's message accurately and to the speaker's satisfaction.

When inviting feedback from your listeners, never use words like 'Any questions?'. Rarely will listeners admit to having listened poorly, so they are unlikely to respond to such a question. Unfortunately, we hear this kind of question often in our story-telling organisations. In any kind of briefing, a more appropriate way of checking the understanding of listeners is to say something like 'Okay, let's go over this one more time to be sure you've got the story straight. What's the first thing you'll need to do?'

Competent story-listeners will be able to pick out the main point of the stories they hear. As they listen, they not only try to remember specific facts or details but they also construct an umbrella view of the story. When asked what the story they have just heard was about, they can summarise it in a succinct sentence:

> - Joanne assures me that she would have finished the report on time had the computer not been down for so long.
> - The bottom line is that the management must reduce the company's expenditure on travel by 20 per cent in the next 12 months.
> - Some staff in human resource management will be transferred to the sales division after they have been retrained.
> - As from next year, employees will no longer receive reduced home loan rates.

A final point—good story-listeners learn from the stories they hear. For example, after hearing the story they can do something which they couldn't do beforehand. Peter Senge has suggested that learning requires metanoia, or 'a shift of the mind'.[12] Just hearing a story without being changed somehow by the experience is the very opposite of metanoia or true learning. Thus, the story-telling organisation, like the learning organisation, encourages people to learn so that they can become more creative human beings.

Of all interpersonal communication skills, listening is probably regarded by the majority of trainers and human resource developers as the most essential for communicative competence. There is no point in telling stories to people who don't know how to listen to them. In Chapter 6 we shall see how managers can develop their listening skills through appropriate training and development.

Summary

There are many different kinds of stories told and heard in organisations. An organisation without stories is an organisation where people don't communicate with each other. When people don't communicate, the organisation falls apart. That's why it's useful to think of your organisation as 'a story-telling organisation'. Using the analogy of a human body, we have seen that story-telling organisations can be described as sick or healthy, depending on the state of the 'body's' lifeblood—its stories. The overarching motive behind story-telling is to experience and thus to harmonise with the life and culture of one's organisation. Everyone in an organisation is a story-teller, in that all people have some story to tell about themselves or their experiences.

We discovered the various ways by which stories are communicated in organisations. Regardless of whether they are written, told in person or communicated non-verbally, stories are the tools for meaning-making. Senior managers who want to share their visions with their staff craft their stories in such a way that the staff can make sense of the vision. At all levels of the organisation, however, stories are told, listened to and interpreted. This is all part of meaning-making.

Three important points emerged about the skills of story-telling. Firstly, good story-tellers help listeners construct meanings about the story they are experiencing. Secondly, skilled story-tellers try to build on their listeners' existing knowledge and understandings, by using analogies, comparisons and metaphors. There will be more discussion of metaphors in Chapter 4. And, thirdly, good story-tellers involve their audience. The skill components of effective story-listening included the ability to suspend judgment, the ability to make reflective responses (empathy) and the ability to give accurate feedback to the story-teller.

While some of the stories told in organisations become enduring myths, many stories have a short lifespan because they are about specific happenings of the moment. In Part II of *Myth-makers and Story-tellers* our attention is drawn to myths and their impact on organisational life and culture.

the organisational myth

3

the nature and purpose of organisational myths

Never take any notice of anonymous letters, unless you get a few thousand on the same subject.
Sir Robert Menzies

Now that we know what a story-telling organisation is, it's time to consider some of the most powerful stories told—organisational myths. In this chapter we take a bird's eye view of the world of organisational myth. We'll discover what kinds of myths can be found in the story-telling organisation. We'll find out why these myths originate, and how they survive or decline.

Of the many heroes of ancient Attica, Theseus is possibly the most colourful and dramatic. Minos, the powerful King of Crete, demanded from the Athenians a tribute, payable every seven years. The tribute was made up of seven young women and seven young men, to be sent to Crete unarmed and to be cast into the Palace Labyrinth where dwelt the Minotaur, a terrifying monster, half beast and half human. Minos agreed that if the sacrificial victims ever succeeded in killing the Minotaur, they would be allowed to return to their homeland.

Part II: The organisational myth

On the third occasion that 14 young Athenians were forced to set sail for Crete, Prince Theseus, son of the Athenian ruler, Aegeus, determined to take his place as one of the seven young men. Aegeus gave Theseus two sails, one black and one white. The black sail was to be used for the journey to Crete, symbolising the deathly nature of the expedition. The white sail was to be brought out for the return journey if Theseus had been successful in slaying the Minotaur.

When the Athenians arrived in Crete they were taken to the Palace, where Theseus met Minos' daughter, Ariadne. They fell in love, and Ariadne agreed to assist Theseus, giving him a ball of thread so that he would not lose his way in the Labyrinth. In return for her help, Theseus promised to marry her and return with her to Athens—if he succeeded in killing the Minotaur.

Theseus fulfilled his duty to the Athenian people by slaying the Minotaur and escaping the Labyrinth. However, according to one version of the legend, he left Crete while Ariadne was sleeping, and she awoke to find herself abandoned and heartbroken. She was comforted by other women on the island, and eventually died giving birth to Theseus' child. Meanwhile, the Prince returned to Attica, so jubilant and exhausted from his labours that he forgot to replace the black sail of mourning with the white sails of triumph. Waiting on the cliffs for his son's return, Aegeus was so grief-stricken at the sight of the black sail that he fell from the cliff and died. With the shadow of this tragedy cast over him, Theseus commenced his reign as regent of Attica.

This ancient myth is the dramatic expression of important themes that teach and guide its hearers in the lessons of life. There is, for example, a strong theme of sacrifice—that of the young Athenians, and particularly Aegeus' sacrifice of his son. There are familiar themes of monster-slaying and heroism typified in Theseus' clash with the Minotaur. There are further themes of doomed passion, such as Ariadne's, and the tragic theme of parental anguish, when Aegeus mistakenly believes that his son has been killed.

Although we are considering a very ancient myth here, these themes still have strong parallels in our lives today. They may not appear literally, but there will always be symbolic monsters like the Minotaur that we must face from time to time, and there will be heroic individuals to step forth as champions of our freedom within the human systems of which we are a part. Our managers at work can be like parent-figures, full of pride for our triumphs and agonising over our mistakes and defeats. Psychologically and morally, there are powerful comparisons that can be made between the themes of primitive myths and the myths that emerge and grow in today's organisations. These themes may be detectable in a variety of metaphors, which provide alternative ways of interpreting what takes place in our workplaces. In this chapter, therefore, we probe the fascinating mysteries of how myths form, and the shape they take in our organisational lives.

The nature of myth

In the language of Homer and the Greek poets, 'mythos' meant 'word' or 'tale'. 'Logos' also means 'speech' or 'word' in Greek. Thus, 'mythology' is the science of 'words about words'. Northrop Frye, the famous literary critic, suggested that this mythology or study of words about words provides 'new directions from old'.[1] Mythology unlocks our mental sets. The myth of Theseus and the Minotaur, for example, describes a hero who must descend into darkness and uncertainty to do battle with his monster, held to safety only by a fragile string (provided by the love of Ariadne). His duty to his father and his people demands that he find a way to achieve the 'impossible'—that he navigate a way through the Labyrinth and defeat the Minotaur. In this battle, traditional bravery and a sword are insufficient, and it is the love of Ariadne, and her clever solution to the problem of the maze, that help Theseus to triumph. His abandonment of Ariadne and his child is mirrored in, and punished by, his own father's death.

Myths can do what our tendency to think in linear ways cannot do—put us in touch with alternative ways of examining our world. Joseph Campbell, the great authority on myth, identified four functions of primitive myths:[2]

- myths provide a sense of awe and mystery about people's worlds
- myths show people the shape of their universe
- myths support and legitimise cultural values and the social order
- myths teach us how to live in our world.

These functions apply not only to primitive or cultural myths but also to organisational myths. The difference between the external world and the world of an organisation is essentially a matter of scale. Organisations that are not too inward-looking and that are in touch with the external environment are really small-scale replicas of the world at large. There was once a pharmaceutical manufacturing company, which was directed by the nation's government to produce chemicals for use in warfare. Every person in that organisation—from the CEO to the assembly line workers—refused to comply, because their shared mission was to preserve and enhance life, and not to destroy it. This story is gradually developing into a powerful myth demonstrating that people within systems can shape their universe and legitimise the values and social order characterising that universe. In addition, the myth offers an appropriate way to live in this world, and in so doing fills us with a sense of respect for the way this organisation fulfilled its mission.

Myths can have simple beginnings. They can originate from 'tales' or 'yarns'. Tales are stories about real or imaginary events and people. As we have already noted, tales are often told informally in casual places like coffee houses or bars—they help to 'pass the time'. 'Yarns' can be short stories or chats or they can be long tales of adventure. Australians often tend to associate yarns with people from the Outback. Some years ago, a series of brief ten-minute episodes was made for Australian television. The series was named 'The Yarns of Billy Borker' and captured the 'masculine' culture of the Australian outback. Billy Borker would sip his beer as he recounted anecdotes about unforgettable people and happenings.

In some situations, the word 'tale' carries a negative connotation, as in 'it's a tale that's hard to believe' or 'telling tales'. Nevertheless, as one of the qualities of myth is its surrounding mystery, it is not hard to see how some myths grow out of improbable or unbelievable tales. Eskimos are quite comfortable with improbability—Eskimo story-tellers claim that they are not actually crafting their stories but that it is their ancestors' wisdom that speaks through them. Some of the tales may not be what Eskimos today want to hear but they are part of the collective wisdom of Eskimo culture.

While it may seem that many 'primitve' myths are essentially elaborations of fictitious supposition, the myths that are handed down from generation to generation are preserved as a legacy of truth. There is no foolproof way of authenticating myths or stories emanating from bygone days. Acceptance of the myth is very much a matter of faith or belief. Religious myths certainly fall into this category. As Paul the Apostle wrote in the tenth chapter of his letter to the Hebrews: 'Faith is the substance of things hoped for, the evidence of things not seen.' So, myths may or may not have a basis in fact, but they are remembered and acted on as though they represent truth and reality.

Many contemporary myths in Western culture, however, seem to have a basis in fantasy and concocted reality. The Superman myth, for example, is based on a fictitious person who represents the cherished values of an entire nation and society—'truth, justice and the American way'. Although Superman can leap buildings in a single bound or stop locomotives with one hand, he is a mortal who can be fatally weakened by a fragment of the mineral kryptonite from his own destroyed planet. One of the successes of modern myths like this one is that story-listeners can identify with the human qualities of superheroes, even though these imaginary characters can do things of which no ordinary people are capable.

Myths when expanded and elaborated upon can become sagas or epics. Epics are lengthy narratives about heroic achievements and were traditionally told or written in an elevated or poetic style. Homer's *Iliad* and *Odyssey* are some of the best known examples of epics. Sagas, too, are narratives or legends of heroic deeds but, unlike epics, they were derived from medieval Icelandic or Norse works and are typically associated with prose rather than with poetry. They often relate the story of a family, sometimes over several generations. Creators of modern sagas include James Michener, author of *The Source* and *Hawaii*, Leon Uris, who wrote *Exodus* and *Mila 18*, and Margaret Mitchell, creator of *Gone With The Wind*. Some sagas have become the inspiration for musicals and operas. Richard Wagner composed a cycle of operas based on the saga of Siegfried, legendary prince of the lower Rhine region and hero of the *Nibelungenlied*. Similarly, Giuseppe Verdi, the nineteenth century Italian composer, wrote operas based on sagas about historical figures like the Babylonian king, Nebuchadnezzar and the tragic Egyptian heroine, Aida.

What are organisational myths?

Myths reveal to us the secrets of our environment and show us the possibilities of deeper understandings about life, nature and spirituality. In practical terms, myths enable us to penetrate our organisational cultures. With new and profound insights into the culture of our professional worlds, we can all learn strategies for coping with difficulties and for reducing uncertainties we may have once had.

When a body of myths is formed in an organisation, it is called a 'mythology'. Organisational mythologies stem from the stimulation of people's imaginations, which are in turn inspired by the organisation's energies and activities. With each new body, there is the possibility of a distinctive new mythology. In other words, each organisation can have its own collection of stories or mythology.

Some people believe that stories about organisations originate externally, and circulate largely by word-of-mouth. For example, shoppers develop impressions of the quality of customer service at department stores. These impressions are communicated as stories to other shoppers. In time, many shoppers will have heard the same story. If the original experience was of poor customer service, the retelling of that experience will predispose all the story-listeners and new story-tellers to believe that department store X doesn't care about its customers. As the story spreads, belief begins to turn to 'fact'. And this is when a myth is born.

A good example is the myth surrounding Harrods, the London department store famous for selling the very best of everything. You name it, they'll get it. A giraffe? An ultralight glider? Plover's eggs? No problem—just about anything of exceptional quality, and which smacks of English aristocracy, can be obtained at Harrods. Because it sells the best of everything, Harrods will not tolerate even the most minor detractions from its image of gentility and perfection. It's a department store that will even eject the rich or famous for not meeting its dress code—Jason Donovan was shown the door for wearing torn jeans. So Harrods has a public meaning larger than its 'department store' category. The myth of Harrods is constantly retold in fashion magazines, social columns and in-flight reading matter.

What about Bill Gates, the twentieth century's eccentric Zeus perched on the Mount Olympus of technology? His besting of the monolithic IBM at the tender age of 19 and founding of Microsoft have left him one of the world's richest men, and the subject of endless rumour, speculation and mythologising. In Australia, a similar myth surrounds Dick Smith, the founder of an empire of affordable electronic goods. The myth surrounding Dick Smith, however, is not specific to his electronic design, production and sales company, now owned and run by others. Dick Smith stands out as an adventurer, aviator and explorer, a founder of the *Australian Geographic* magazine, entrepreneur and philanthropist. Legendary characters like Gates and Smith are what John Lonergan calls 'paradigm people', or leaders, in the 1990s 'chaos decade'— visionaries who welcome unconventional thinking and who are prepared to seize upon new opportunities as they present themselves.[3] Such prominent myth-makers are known today well beyond the spheres in which they first demonstrated their abilities.

Most organisational myths, however, originate from *within* the system. An organisation's mythology has a harmonising effect on its members. A type of collective wisdom develops, enabling individuals to understand where they fit into the scheme of things.

Every mythology has its own pantheon of god-like creatures and demigods—mythologies grow up around the stories that tell of their exploits, of the creation and destruction of the worlds associated with them.

Myths about an organisation's pioneers to whom are attributed the company's present successes or problems can be told with a veil of mystery. People of the past become giants or visionary prophets or the unbridled monsters and villains responsible for present circumstances. Often the principal players or characters in these myths are associated with a single visionary or catastrophic action or decision. There is a story of a well-known gemstone merchant company, which we will call 'Jewel in the Sun'. It started as a small family business and grew into the largest national retailer of design jewellery. The two directors, a husband and wife team, sank their life savings into one impressive advertisement for their company. The gamble paid off. Within weeks they were getting so much business they had to find larger premises for sales and office space. Several new staff were hired. When their jewellery designer won an international award soon after, the business was secure as a rock. The cost of the original advertisement was $250. Twenty years later the company was bought out for over $100 million.

This story has a rather awesome feel to it. We are left wondering what would have happened if the advertisement had not been originally placed. The 'Jewel in the Sun' myth reveals the enormous potential perceived by the company's shrewd proprietors. This was the shape of things that could come and that did transpire. This myth showed that the company's success depended on resolute courage, risk-taking and lots of hard work on the part of the owners and employees. These were the values which best fitted this commercial enterprise. A lesson we could draw from this myth is that the formula for success in setting up a new business does not invariably require huge amounts of backing capital but entrepreneurial skill and dedication.

Perhaps a more familiar myth is the one associated with Lee Iacocca, CEO of the US Chrysler Motor Corporation, who pulled his company out of financial crisis—partly through his symbolic and heroic act of reducing his salary to $1. When employees at Chrysler learned of his personal sacrifice, the story became part of the organisation's culture, transforming it into a great myth. The effect was to bond the workers of Chrysler together with a common purpose in adversity. Now Iacocca is remembered as an exemplary team-builder and creator of a successful team culture in his organisation.

Balancing dualities

Some mythologies in our world of today tend to be based on dualities or opposites. In line with the 'yin and yang' of Eastern culture, our mythologies emphasise the difference between good and evil, right and wrong, heaven and hell. These opposites can be compared to a set of balance scales: on the one side sits good and on the other, evil. Myths may develop when an imbalance between forces is not righted, particularly when negative forces appear to be stronger than positive ones.

Common dualities in our organisational mythologies		
worker participation	vs	managerial decision-making
promotion by merit	vs	promotion by seniority
experience	vs	qualifications
task-sharing	vs	task-delegation
consultation	vs	giving orders
strategic planning	vs	crisis management
financial incentive	vs	job satisfaction
risk	vs	security
ethical behaviour	vs	'dog eat dog' tactics

One means of accounting for people's tendencies to think in these 'either/ or' terms derives from the basic mythological theme that 'in the beginning there was unity out of which grew separation'. In some early myths, for example, the separation of male and female occurred some time after creation, when people were unisexual. Similarly, in many organisational mythologies, the emergence of 'evil forces' in an organisation's culture may be first noticed at some point far beyond the organisation's original establishment.

Keeping myths alive

When myths are kept alive in organisations, the system should thrive. Skilled and artistic story-tellers keep myths alive through their creative narratives. Artists also work hard to make their works enduring. The mythologisation of organisations is an artistic and creative enterprise: the artist's creation is continually brought alive through story retelling. Thus, listeners also have an important part to play in keeping myths alive. In some instances, myths are kept alive simply because the hero or villain continues to perform heroic or villainous deeds. Original myths are reinforced when new actions build on already mythologised behaviours.

In today's world, myth-making and myth-interpretation is more difficult than it has been in the past. Because myths take time to develop, needing periods of relative stability in human systems, and because change seems to be the only constant in organisations these days, few stories become myths. Constant change is demythologising our world. Today, the failure to generate new myths has created a void in our culture.

The life cycle of a myth

The gradual disappearance of myths in today's world suggests that myths have a finite lifetime. David Boje hypothesised that organisational myths progress through 'a myth-making life cycle' of four stages.[4] In the first stage—*development*—the myth is created and guides organisational decision-making and strategy. The *maturation* stage follows when the myth becomes 'solid'. At this stage, the myth and the organisation become inseparable in people's minds. For example, one simply can't think of certain media corporations without relating these to myths about barons like Rupert Murdoch or Kerry Packer.

Part II: The organisational myth

In the third stage—*decline*—myths lose their relevance to the enterprise or the organisation. The myth can even begin to harm the organisation's capacity to address changing needs or a changing environment. Some organisations may try to find ways of bolstering the declining myth. More usually, however, people develop new, competing myths or stories. This is also known as 'myth split'. The fourth stage—*reformulation*—is a time of 'myth shift', where the dominant myth structure breaks down. There may be accompanying tension and conflict between old and new myths, and between alternative new myths competing for dominance. Often a change in leadership seems necessary at this point. Below is an example to illustrate the myth-making life cycle.

The case of the failed entrepreneurs

Over the past ten to 15 years, Australians have witnessed the rise and fall of a number of prominent businesspeople. Christopher Skase is now living in Spain, Alan Bond now has a comparatively low profile as a public figure and Harry M. Miller appears to be slowly rising like a phoenix out of the ashes after his brief period of imprisonment for his part in the collapse of a financial enterprise. In these cases, we can see how the myth life cycle may be applied to the fluctuating fortunes of such entrepreneurs.

From Stage 1, these businesspeople battle to become prominent public figures, often engaged in activities furthering the common good of Australia and Australians. Among other things, Alan Bond, for example, sponsored the syndicate that successfully captured the America's Cup yachting trophy in the early 1980s.

At Stage 2 the myth becomes 'solid'. In Bond's case, a new university on the Queensland Gold Coast, predictably named Bond University, is established. The myth-maker and the organisation are now inseparable in the public's mind. During Stage 3, doubts are cast upon the credibility of the myth-maker, predominantly over complicity in failed financial transactions. A period of prolonged litigation and legal activity sees the weakening of the power of the myth surrounding our entrepreneur.

In the final stage the myth is destroyed. Alan Bond is imprisoned for three months, Harry M. Miller for less than a year, and Skase escapes to Spain, avoiding extradition. The former high-fliers and myth-makers are no longer heroic figures. Eventually new myths will emerge, as new heroes become associated with these businesses and enterprises.

This example shows that even in a relatively short space of time organisational myths have a life cycle. In the space of a generation or less, the early successes of these business entrepreneurs have been offset by the blunders and miscalculations of ambition. The time intervals between the stages may vary from myth-maker to myth-maker but progression through the cycle remains the same for all of them. The power and duration of certain myths depends to some extent on the ability of the myth-makers to undertake their heroic journey without faltering.

Myths can shape the culture of organisations. Through myths, we can form images of the organisation and judge whether it is healthy or ailing. They tell us about the people who are saving the organisation and those who are bringing it down. In our organisations, myths also reveal to us whether the gods are smiling or whether their wrath has been incurred. From these revelations we can obtain a pretty good idea of whether there is hope or despair for the survival and future of the organisation. We are now beginning to see why there are myths in organisations. Let's give this question more attention.

Why do myths exist in organisations?

Some of the reasons for myths developing in organisations have already been hinted at. Other important reasons are that myths support rituals, that they communicate values and that they help leaders to envisage the future.

Myths support rituals

Religious myths provide members of religious organisations with clear and definable rituals. In Christian churches, for example, the ritual of communion—where members of the congregation take a sip of sacramental wine and a small piece of bread or wafer—is based on the story of the Last Supper Christ had with his disciples before he sacrificed his 'body and blood' in his crucifixion. The church ritual of kneeling or genuflecting symbolises a person's subservience to the will and power of God. The practice of bowing or of prostrating oneself is also common in some Eastern religions. Through participating in rituals people re-enact myths. Rituals help keep the myths alive and myths confer meaning upon the rituals.

Part II: The organisational myth

In a similar way, many of our organisational rituals are founded on beliefs which have been mythologised. For example, the practice of managing by walking around (MBWA) is based on the belief that managers are most effective when they are not remote from those they lead. So, for many managers moving around the organisation, communicating and spending time with subordinates has become a regular if not a daily ritual. All kinds of rituals are based on beliefs that it is good or proper to do these things. In turn, these beliefs are strengthened when they have stories formed around them. The creation and the retelling of myths give meaning to ritualised behaviour and convert the belief from a hypothetical piece of wisdom to a reality. Some of the personal rituals managers observe in their working lives might include:

- joining staff for morning or afternoon coffee or tea breaks
- celebrating people's birthdays, engagements and the birth of their children
- having parties on occasions like the Melbourne Cup and St Patrick's Day
- giving of 'silly' gifts to staff at Christmas
- having drinks with staff after work on Fridays.

As we can see, some of these rituals are performed to say 'thank you' to a colleague or to give recognition to someone's performance or efforts. Other rituals like celebrating birthdays or having parties have the effect of boosting morale in the organisation. Similarly, recognising and rewarding staff for their hard work can contribute immeasurably to a positive working climate and to the quality of life in the organisation. Happy times are remembered by those who have shared them and become stories to be retold. Repetitions of pleasant memories can convert these stories to myths where the managers are given attributes like 'caring for their staff like no one else has done' or 'being generous without any provocation from colleagues'.

Myths communicate values

Through myths people's values are communicated and clarified. Myths are the carriers of organisational values. Values are extremely important. Regardless of whether we mean the values of individuals or the values of a

The nature and purpose of organisational myths

group or an entire organisation, these values determine how people in systems will perform.[5] The myths in healthy organisations usually promote values like hard work, dedication, service, respect for colleagues and clients, efficiency and quality performance. Often the most prized values in an organisation are captured in the organisation's mission statement or motto.

Mottoes that reveal an organisation's values

For the most important person in the world—you!
 —*National Mutual Life Association*

Putting people first
 —*New South Wales government*

For banking tailored to your needs
 —*National Australia Bank*

We throw ourselves at your feet
 —*Mathers Shoes*

City Ford says 'yes' more often
 —*City Ford Motors*

Committed to the fine art of old fashioned service
 —*Trade Winds Travel Inn Hotel*

For that personal service that money can't buy
 —*Ryde Travel Centre*

The best in any case
 —*Paklite Travel Goods*

Drives your dollar further
 —*Budget Rent-A-Car*

Where the food matches the view
 —*Summit restaurant*

Driven by innovation
 —*Subaru*

There's no other store like David Jones
 —*David Jones*

These examples show how a cleverly conceived motto can appeal to the needs and values of members of the receiving system. Clients and customers are

Part II: The organisational myth

often attracted by claims of unique services or products. In part, this explains the success of the David Jones department store motto. The implication here is that you can get from David Jones what you may not be able to get anywhere else, including a unique atmosphere. Subaru is also implying a unique approach. Is the implication that other motor vehicles may be driven, not by innovation, but rather by convention?

People want to be associated with the best. That's why Paklite has been so successful. Words like 'best' and 'better' are very seductive. Even when these words are not used directly, a message of being the best can be conveyed. The Summit restaurant, for example, is known to have spectacular views. By saying that the food is as good as the view, the claim to being superior is subtly established.

In some of the other mottoes, the theme is quality customer service. Prominent financial and insurance services companies like National Mutual provide a message of reassurance to potential clients. National Mutual emphasises the importance of personal attention to the needs of individual clients. Similarly, National Australia Bank (NAB) professes to cater to the personal needs of its customers. In the motto of Mathers Shoes, the same value of service is put more humorously.

Other organisations like Budget Rent-A-Car emphasise the value of affordability and economy. The values of an organisation tell us a lot about the health and culture of the organisation. Myths enable these values to be brought into the open and to become part of the cultural experience of the organisation.

Not all values are worn on an organisation's shirtsleeves. What is *professed* may not reflect the *actual* values of an organisation. For example, customer service is often part of the professed mission or goal of organisations, yet attention to customer needs is often ignored in these places. How many times have you had to ask directly, 'Is there someone here who can help me?' after a frustrating time attempting to catch the attention of salespeople conducting private conversations? It is not uncommon for people to extoll the virtues of teamwork after having 'stabbed a co-worker in the back'. By tapping into the myths, and thereby the culture, of an organisation, we can get a 'feel' for it, warts and all. This means we can detect not only what is actually happening, but also what should be happening when we come into contact with an organisation's mythology.

The nature and purpose of organisational myths

Without myths, an organisation can quickly become lifeless—a machine missing a soul. So, myths are central to survival and happiness in our organisations. Myths are used to find the organisation's heartbeat and pulse. Myths are required to map and guide us through our organisations. As members, we replenish our energy from the vitality that myths bring.

Interpreting the past, envisaging the future

Interpreting myth is not simply a matter of learning from history what mistakes not to repeat. There is a timeless quality about myths which enables us not only to view the past and present but also to envisage the future. Joseph Campbell noted that typical opening and closing lines of myths and legends 'set apart from the common world the timeless, placeless realm of faerie'.[6] We all know stories that begin with 'Once upon a time . . .', 'In the kingdom of good King X . . .', 'A thousand years ago tomorrow . . .' or 'Long, long ago, when . . .'.

In organisations, the science of words about words enables us to catch glimpses of our future professional world. Sometimes, the myths are supported by factual data—such as the past five years' sales or production growth curves, showing trends for the immediate future. But the glimpse of the future need not only be based on data-based trends of this kind. Visionary leaders use mythology to 'get a feel' for the future. It is difficult to explain this in material terms, but the visionary leader is sensitive to all kinds of information and sensory inputs. Visionary leaders are highly observant, taking in and interpreting everything they can know through their five basic senses as well as from a 'sixth sense', which may well differentiate them from people without vision. That sixth sense, possibly intuition, will feed on myths and acts like a radar to keep the leader in very close touch with a timeless world.

Mythological interpretation means entering some darkly wooded 'virgin territory', where the explorer's experience is totally original. By closely observing all the natural signs and features of the forest, the leader-as-mythologist plots a path through unknown places. Once the other side of the difficult terrain is reached, the leader has acquired a new repertoire of interpreted experiences which can benefit others in the organisation. The process of facing and understanding the unknown so that others will be able to do the same is the mark of a hero. Navigators of the past—Christopher Columbus, Ferdinand Magellan, Vasco de Gama, James Cook—are role-models for organisational leaders. Each of them went through the process of learning from the unknown.

Not all managers learn to traverse the unexplored territory of the organisational psyche successfully. One of the problems is that some of today's organisations are becoming 'demythologised'. The assumption some managers make is that there is no more 'unknown'—everything has been explained and interpreted. These managers have surrounded themselves with material practicalities that obstruct their view of a better world. Decisions are made on the formulaic basis of 'good management practice' rather than creatively. The result is that often weak or inappropriate decisions are made, after which dissatisfaction and an 'us and them' culture develops. The organisational climate can become very negative and counterproductive.

Roland Barthes noted that for many of today's people 'tomorrow's positivity is entirely hidden by today's negativity'.[7]

Sources of organisational myths

Organisational myths may be told not by the fireside but in formal documents where information is kept factual. Reports of organisational audits, for example, may tell the story of a hero's achievements in a kind of officialese. The authors of the report are unlikely to wax poetic or lyrical over the exploits of the hero they have identified because the language of the report is designed for factual accuracy rather than for the reader's elevation, spiritual transport or inspiration. Myths about organisational heroes may also originate from key statements in an organisation's chronicles or annals. These statements, often hinting at some heroic deed, become the foundation stones to build myths. Below are some key statements that could be expanded into organisational myths:

The nature and purpose of organisational myths

- The company vice-president responsible for sales, Ida Bortitt, has helped to generate an amount of business and turnover such that for the next triennium not only will there be no retrenchments but it is also anticipated that there will be an expansion of the company's workforce by 10 per cent in sales and 5 per cent in administration.
- The company quality assurance executive, Munn E. Saver, introduced recyclable internal office envelopes thus cutting stationery expenditure by almost 50 per cent over the next financial year.
- Staff Development's newest team member, Emma Trainer, turned in-house training into fun by running all training courses off-site at a holiday resort.
- The Occupational Health and Safety Department Head, Noah Riske, organised fitness classes for all staff before work in the mornings. Since the first class, the number of people requiring workers' compensation for work-related illnesses has dropped to virtually zero.
- The award for outstanding customer service went to the inner city branch of the You Mamma's Pizza chain of stores. Julio and Tomasina Pepperoni, the store's franchise managers, were the first to commence a home delivery service for customers within a five kilometre radius.

Other examples of potential organisational myths can be found in written performance reviews or appraisals, annual reports, and in records of board and committee meetings.

A special example of publicly telling an organisational myth can be found in some university graduation ceremonies where a distinguished person may be awarded an honorary degree. Prior to the actual award of the testamur, a senior member of the university's executive, like a vice-chancellor or dean, typically reads a citation of the recipient's lifetime achievements—a documented saga. Publicly granting an honour to someone in an organisation can therefore involve the telling of a saga.

You can get an idea of what an organisational saga is like from the following brief summary of an organisational myth, which would undoubtedly be expanded through story-telling.

Part II: The organisational myth

A saga of appalling promotion

In January 1993, Kay Osse, was appointed to Federal Life Assurance as the state human resources department manager. Kay's new department had nine staff members—five were in the training and development section, three were in personnel (recruitment and administration) and one person looked after human resources planning. The ninth member was the general administrative assistant and receptionist, who was intended to give support to all staff in the department.

Kay was instructed by her supervisor, Mr Bigg-Klymer, a divisional manager reporting to the branch executive, that she should develop a strategic and business plan for her department, in line with the company's mission statement. Mr Bigg-Klymer also told Kay that the branch executive members of Federal Life regarded her department as a model of efficiency and initiative. Other departments at Federal Life were being directed to follow the example of the human resources department.

The department was held in high regard because the training and development section was under the leadership of a highly creative and astute internal consultant, Ms Senn O'Wight. Senn expected her staff to spend time talking to people in other parts of the organisation because their real needs had to be identified before providing them with services. Within a year of Senn's appointment, the organisation of training and development had been completely revolutionised. Staff from divisions were clamouring for more training on the grounds that the training they had received so far had been thoroughly beneficial and relevant to their needs.

Eventually, Senn approached Kay with a request for more staff to handle the internal demand for training. Kay did not react with enthusiastic support. In fact, Kay did not like Senn. She felt threatened by Senn and her obvious talent for making things happen. So, Kay began to develop her strategic plan, which for some time she did not share with her staff. Her idea was to expand the administrative support staff of her department by cutting down the number of specialists in high profile areas like training and development. Secretly, she was determined to undermine the success and achievements of Senn. Kay was simply jealous. She wanted no one to shine but herself.

Eventually, staff began to wonder why Kay was hinting about a rightsizing strategy at her infrequent team meetings. Gradually, it became clear that Kay was building her empire by cutting down the opportunities for other staff members to take the initiative.

The nature and purpose of organisational myths

Senn was not only refused the extra number of training consultants she was hoping to recruit, but was also asked to reduce her training staff by one so that a new position in personnel administration could be created. Kay said that she regretted this but that the order was coming from the branch executive. The staff knew that wasn't true—the branch executive tended to be guided by the advice of divisional managers. Kay had been drumming up support for her strategy from her supervisor, Bigg-Klymer.

As far as Senn was concerned, the writing was on the wall. As long as Kay was in charge, Senn would never have support to make the training team as successful as possible. During the next six months, Senn was asked to downsize her section by a further two staff members. This brought her section down to two people. When Senn was offered an executive management position at a rival financial institution she left Federal Life. Her departure gave Kay the excuse to close down the training section entirely and retrain the training consultants for roles in personnel administration.

Throughout the company, staff began to see the human resources department as a hindrance rather than as a help to them. Kay insisted that all future requests from staff in other departments be made on newly designed forms. Red tape quadrupled. Branch executive members received increasing numbers of complaints about Kay's department, particularly regarding the poor service to other departments in the organisation. Line managers who saw a need for training and developing their staff made urgent pleas to branch executive for budget supplements to recruit their own trainers.

As staff morale plummeted, the branch executive sought advice from head office. The group manager for human resources advised that in future all human resource functions would be centralised at head office. This meant that all state branches would be required to close down their human resource departments. A small number of staff would be given the opportunity to be redeployed. The remainder would be given redundancy packages. It was Kay's duty to oversee the process.

In the next three months, three of the remaining staff took up equivalent positions in other organisations. The rest were given redundancy packages. Kay had been seen to be very efficient in dismantling her department, without spilling too much blood, and she was promoted to assistant group manager for human resources. She brought with her the reputation for being the most efficient hatchet woman the organisation had ever seen. Everyone knew that she was a highly political creature with unbridled ambition.

Part II: The organisational myth

> After two years in her new role, Kay was moved sideways from her position. She was given the new title of 'special projects manager'. The national executive members were unanimous in saying they could not entrust Kay with a position where she would become jealous of the successes of her subordinates. In effect, Kay was now a manager without portfolio and in danger of being retrenched.
>
> Kay will always be remembered as the person who turned strength into weakness and success into failure by converting what was once a successful enterprise into an unsupported white elephant within the organisation. Even more, she will be remembered for being promoted for destroying her department.

Obviously, the particular story-tellers will add details of their own. There will be specific pieces of information, anecdotes and interpretations accumulating in the telling and retelling of the story until it assumes the proportions of a saga. In time, the Kay Osse myth, therefore, will become part of the folklore and culture of the organisation. Future generations of workers will speak of 'doing a Kay job' without ever having met Kay. 'Kay' will have become a symbol of destruction and of rewarded mediocrity.

At least three 'morals' or lessons will be learned and remembered from the Kay myth. First, in this company, creativity is less important than being politically aware. Senn may have been the most talented employee but Kay was rewarded because she played politics better than Senn.

Secondly, when executive members are out of touch with those at the 'sharp end' of things, they tend to rely on the line of managers reporting immediately to them. If these managers are influenced by people like Kay, they are likely to support recommendations that are both counterproductive and injurious to the wellbeing of the organisation. Poor leadership from the top begets poor leadership down the line of management.

Thirdly, we must remember that the Kays in any organisation will realise their selfish aims if no quality assurance mechanism is in place to counteract their ill-conceived actions. Because Senn and her training team devoted their energies to their jobs, they did not become involved in the shadow side of the organisation. All the behind-the-scenes jockeying for power would have diverted their concentration from training to in-house adversarial communication.

The nature and purpose of organisational myths

The Kay myth is based on a real-life story. It is a lengthy story about the triumph of mediocrity over talent. This may seem like a negative topic for a myth. Nevertheless, it does provide a striking illustration of how pushy and ambitious people with no talent are sometimes more likely to be listened to and rewarded by their managers than talented people who get on with their job without seeking publicity for their achievements.

So, as we can see, not all myths are about heroes. Indeed, some myths are about anti-heroes like Kay. Today, while Federal Life continues to bumble along after a string of poor decisions and errors by its 'leaders', at one branch the person most remembered as regrettably lost to the organisation was Senn. A myth is gradually developing about the heroic and legendary exploits of Senn and her team when training and development was at its zenith in Federal Life.

The creativity of the organisational myth is largely in how it is conceived and told. When the subject of the organisational epic is some beloved or well-remembered pioneer in the company, and when the story is told by someone who once knew the legendary person, the narrative will very likely have a strong emotional flavour. Story-listeners could expect to hear words like 'I remember well the time when . . .' or 'In those days, she was always known for her generosity to the workers'.

Some organisational myths, however, occasionally may appear in published papers. For example, obituaries may contain elaborated statements of strong feeling about the deceased person. There has been a noticeable proliferation of books that chronicle organisational myths, such as John Sculley's journey from Pepsi to Apple Computers, books on Microsoft, on Xerox, on Virgin, on General Electric, on Rupert Murdoch's media empire . . . Other instances of organisational epics can be evidenced in speeches at retirement functions or at 'roasts' where individuals are honoured and remembered for their achievements and/or services.

Organisational epics contain elements of truth and bent reality. Much depends on what the story-teller wants to remember and on how the narrator wants the listener to remember the story. When the story-teller has strong positive feelings and attitudes to the hero, any faults or failings of the honoured person tend to be obscured by the litany of virtues being recounted.

Part II: The organisational myth

Although people have traditionally associated myths with gods, it is true that in classical Greco-Roman mythology many mythical characters have been legendary mortals with extraordinary powers, or superior strength, wit and courage. The heroes include Hercules, who successfully completed 12 superhuman labours, Perseus, the slayer of the Gorgon Medusa, and Theseus, who killed the Minotaur in the Palace Labyrinth of the Cretan King Minos. (In Chapter 4, the slaying or taming of monsters is discussed as a theme central to modern organisational myths.) Organisational myths may originate in short or simple stories but over time can grow into memorable epics or sagas.

Summary

After exploring the power of myth to create sense of our universe by supporting and legitimising personal ideals, cultural values and the social order, we turned our attention to organisational myths. We began our journey into the world of organisational myths by observing that they are special kinds of organisational stories which enable us to gain deeper insights into the life and culture of our organisations. Some myths can develop into epics and sagas—while other organisational stories have a comparatively short lifespan. Myths have a life cycle of four stages, beginning with myth-creation and ending with the generation of new myths.

We also learned that there are organisational myths which can apply to a range of organisations because the heroes of these myths have qualities recognisable in many different environments. Organisational myths do not always appear in poetic and lyrical language—often they are obscured by officialese or buried in formal documents. Chapter 4 outlines some essential components of myths that will assist you in recognising myths where they occur in your organisation.

4

themes, archetypes, heroes and metaphors

It may be that our role on this planet is not to worship God—but to create him.
Arthur C. Clarke

Are the myths we hear and read about in our own organisations anything like those told elsewhere? Who are the heroes and archetypes in our organisational mythologies? What effect do they have on our own story-telling? What is the language of organisational myth? What common metaphors are found in myth-making and story-telling? These are some of the questions to be addressed as the world of myth is probed further.

Themes in organisational myths

According to Clyde Kluckhohn, there are recurrent themes in primitive myths and myth-making.[1] Nearly every religion in our world has myths about the creation of the sun and moon, or earth and sky. These have also been referred to as the first parents and the sun's rays have been responsible for the first impregnation. A creator has moulded the first humans from the earth in the ground. Some managers may be tempted to say 'What do primitive myths have to do with contemporary organisational myths?'. David Boje, a leading scholar in organisational behaviour and story-telling, says that different kinds of myths from various periods of the world's history exist and 'struggle' in the story-telling organisation. He states that three kinds of 'learning discourse' can be found in the story-telling organisation. 'Pre-modern' story-telling is a

> *... mythical and nomadic journey, defending pre-industrial artisan craftsmanship, spirituality, family and a strong sense of community over economic rationality.*[2]

Apart from pre-modern learning discourses, Boje identified 'modern story-telling', preoccupied with issues of capitalism, efficiency, bureaucracy, rationality and technology. Modernist story-tellers see their organisations in terms of 'machine' metaphors. Finally, in 'post-modern' story-telling, themes which have been excluded or marginalised in pre-modern and modern story-telling are picked up. For example, in post-modern story-telling themes like racism, sexism, ecological issues and general political correctness are analysed and 'deconstructed'.

Those who think that the myths of the past have no relevance in today's story-telling organisations have failed to accept the inevitability of previous story-tellers' legacies. Since all three kinds of stories co-exist within the story-telling organisation, it is difficult to understand how one kind could not influence another. Heroes in pre-modern stories, for example, can become archetypes or role-models in modern or post-modern stories. Some mythological themes have lasted for great periods of time and have come to be seen as recurrent, common or applicable in many organisations, and in some cases, even universal.

Creation mythology

Perhaps the most common theme in primitive mythology relates to the creation of our universe. Creation is also a recurrent theme in organisational mythology. The following is an example of an organisational creation myth:

Themes, archetypes, heroes and metaphors

> In 1900 there was an outbreak of bubonic plague in Sydney's docklands and the inner city. This disease was attributed to the importation of infected rats on cargo ships, and the poor standard of maintenance of the wharf and cargo handling areas by their private owners.
>
> As a result the government of the day created the Sydney Harbour Trust. The organisation—whose first employee was a rat catcher—assumed control of the city's wharves and enforced acceptable standards of maintenance and hygiene. In 1936 this organisation was renamed the Maritime Services Board of New South Wales.[3]

Attached to this myth there is also an apocryphal story that before the organisation was renamed, a suggestion had been made to call the organisation the Sydney Harbour Improvement Trust, mainly because of its mission to conserve and make safe the harbour region. Quite unintentionally, the acronym gave an unfortunately contrary impression of the harbour's standard of maintenance and sanitary state. So, the organisation eventually became known as the MSB (Maritime Services Board). This organisational creation story has for some time been included in the induction training courses for MSB staff. In short, it has become part of the culture of the MSB.

Organisational creation myths are often associated with a founder. For example, an advertisement for AV Jennings Homes used the originator of the company, Jennings himself, referring to himself as 'a proud old builder'. The message of the advertisement was that even the person at the top took pride in the quality of home construction by his modern crew of builders. It was almost as though 'God' from on high had given a seal of approval to the work done by those building houses for a divine kingdom on Earth.

The Great Flood . . .

Another dominant and recurring myth has the theme of an old world being destroyed and the corresponding emergence of a new world. The destruction may have coincided with the 'Great Flood'. This is a theme which appears in Biblical, Greco-Roman and Mesopotamian myths, among others. When Zeus decided to destroy the vice-ridden people of the Bronze Age, he sent down a great flood to drown them. Only two people were spared—Deucalion and his wife Pyrrha—because they were not wicked like the rest of humankind. In Akkadian literature, the Gilgamesh Epic has Utanapishtim as the heroic survivor who, on the advice of the water-god, Enki, built a boat to escape a seven-day flood. There are clear parallels between the Deucalion myth, the Epic of Gilgamesh and the familiar *Old Testament* story of Noah and the Ark.

The Flood theme in primitive myths also has its parallel in organisational mythology. Just as the Flood represents a catastrophic time of change in the history of the earth—probably coinciding with some geologically ancient interglacial period—so too, organisations can have their times of upheaval and change. A 'Flood' is a symbol of potential disaster. It connotes devastation and destruction. This is why people use expressions like 'it never rains, but it pours' when they describe a chain of events or circumstances which can inhibit or interfere with the productivity of the system. Quite likely, organisations facing a flood will have a heroic saviour with an ark to keep the company 'afloat'. The deluge of water is also a dramatic symbol of purification—a 'washing away' of old sins and systems so that new life can grow.

. . . and other disasters

In more general terms, 'disaster' is a commonly recurring theme in organisational mythologies. Natural disasters—such as bush fires, volcanic eruptions, earthquakes, droughts, tidal waves, avalanches, hurricanes, typhoons and thunderstorms—can be thought of as 'acts of God'. They can be applied metaphorically to powerful forces impinging on organisational life and survival. We should not forget that disasters can also be perpetrated by people. Poor quality control, inefficient and dishonest work practices, failure to observe occupational health and safety regulations and procedures, and lack of interpersonal communication competence can contribute significantly to entropy—the tendency for an organisation to become disorderly, chaotic and, ultimately, self-destructive.

The disaster theme typically has as its villains the perpetrators of the catastrophe. It may need to be determined whether the disaster occurred accidentally or deliberately. Fires can flare up in conditions of extreme heat and wind—but they can also be deliberately lit by arsonists or be caused by incendiary devices and explosives. When disasters can be attributed to some person(s), another common recurrent theme in organisational myths may emerge—the theme of slaying monsters.

Dragon-slaying

The destruction of a threat in the form of a monster is a theme central to many primitive myths and has been linked with many memorable and legendary heroes. St George and St Michael were famous dragon killers in medieval mythology. In Babylonian mythology, the she-dragon Tiamat, bent on universal destruction, was slain by the divine champion Marduk who was armed with 'matchless weapons'.[4] In modern organisational myths, the dragons may represent oppressive managers who are ultimately destroyed by the oppressed workers or alert superiors. The monster may also be a more symbolic creature—apathy or disloyalty. The following story shows how an organisation can be saved from the clutches of a dragon by a saint or knight in armour.

> Mr Harris Mente made life a misery for every woman at work. As supervisor of the finance division of the company Money for Jam, Harris ruled his empire with an iron fist. He was known for his twisted sense of humour—it was Harris who suggested that the company motto should be 'We have interest in your money'. He also had a reputation as a womaniser. On arrival, every new female employee was warned that her rejection of his advances would predispose him to make life at work intolerable for her.
>
> One day, a new accountant, Ms Abba Cuss, joined the division. Harris asked her to stay back after work and come to his office to review some unexplained accounts. Abba duly stayed back and after some discussion Harris grabbed her and tried to kiss her. Harris soon discovered the futility of assaulting someone with a black belt in judo.
>
> The next day at work, Abba's colleagues asked her how she survived the experience of staying back at Harris' office. 'No problems,' she said. 'You could say that although he fell for me, I didn't fall for him.' As it happened, Harris didn't turn up to work for a week. One story offered to explain his absence was that he had developed some mysterious illness. When he did return, he seemed very subdued. Since that time he has never harrassed any of his female staff. Abba became the most respected and liked person in her division. To all the women on the staff, she was the hero who gave the monster Harris Mente a long overdue lesson in appropriate behaviour towards female workers.

Part II: The organisational myth

The broken home: patricide, matricide and sibling rivalry

In primitive mythology, the theme of parent killing is closely associated with monster slaying. Parent slaying, of course, is only one of several mythological themes linked with family relationships. In primitive mythology, for example, incest was a recurrent theme. 'Family' here need not be taken literally—'being part of the family' is a metaphorical way of saying 'you belong in our team'. New staff members are often not regarded as part of the family until they have proven their loyalty and commitment to the organisation.

Parent-killing

Generally, parents in these myths represent evil, the protagonist's dependence or lack of freedom, and do not always have the best interests of their children at heart. Sometimes, the parent is in a position of power, as in being ruler of a nation. The organisational analogy here is that the father/king or mother/queen is the CEO and the children/subjects in the kingdom are the workforce in the organisation. Here's an example of how the parent-slaying theme might apply to a modern organisation.

> Mr Laius Theban was the tyrannical boss of a large family business. An autocrat, in his early sixties, he enjoyed finding the slightest excuse to put down any of his subordinates for inefficiency or below par performance. His favourite expression was 'you don't get workers today like you used to in the old days'. The only staff member who wasn't really scared of Mr Theban was his adopted son, Eddie Pusse, who was sympathetic to the staff.
>
> Since all members of staff were also shareholders, they were entitled to vote at annual general meetings. Eddie Pusse lobbied his fellow workers and was nominated for chair of the board of directors. In particular, Eddie pledged to put an end to the oppressive and dictatorial management of Laius. He was thus standing in opposition to the present chair, his father, who announced his intention to contest the election. When the vote was put at the annual general meeting, Eddie Pusse won in a landslide.
>
> Laius Theban resigned from the board. His wife Jo Caster, also a board member, announced her support for her son at the meeting. The staff were happy and began to take pride in their work. They wanted to justify the confidence Eddie had placed in them. Under his benevolence, the company prospered—no challenge was issued to his position as chair of the board.

This story shows that the mythical theme of parent-slaying has plenty of relevance and parallels in modern organisational life. Replacing the person who hired you, or someone who has acted as a mentor, may be an inevitable part of organisational change, but it can often produce highly charged emotions.

Sibling rivalry
Both in primitive and modern organisational myths, another commonly found theme about family relationships is sibling rivalry. In the *Bible*, sibling rivalry is a recurrent theme. Cain killed his brother Abel and Jacob deceived his brother Esau in order to obtain the birthright from his father. Even Moses exhorted the Israelites to kill those of their brothers who had strayed from the ways of God to a life of decadence modelled on the behaviour of the Egyptians. The prophet Micah, commenting on the moral decay of his society, predicted that the world was becoming so crime-ridden that people 'all lie in wait for blood; they hunt every man his brother with a net'. Again, in the parable of the Prodigal Son, the hard-working brother of a spendthrift was both angry and jealous because of the lavish welcome his father had given to his homecoming son. In Roman mythology, Romulus, the founder of Rome, killed his brother Remus after a dispute about the location of the city boundary.

Sibling rivalry in organisational myths is usually associated with power contests between feuding or dissenting 'family members'. The usual goal of a power contest is financial monopoly or control over the empire. It is likely that sibling rivalry originates in early childhood and can continue throughout people's lifetimes. Even where sibling relationships are friendly and strongly positive, bad blood can develop if a legacy or inheritance clearly favours one family member over another. In such cases, solid family ties can be transformed into motives for 'getting even' or for assuming the mantle of 'head of the household'.

Sacrifice, salvation and valour
Other recurrent themes in primitive and organisational mythologies are sacrifice, salvation and heroism. In some respects, these three are closely related. For example, all three themes could be associated with resolute and courageous leadership. The mythological hero has to have this quality in

order to fight for the preservation of what is good and right. This fight could involve some sacrifice or the giving of ground, such as closing an unprofitable division. It could also involve manoeuvring oneself into a position of strength and advantage so that the salvation of the organisation or parts of it becomes a distinct possibility. Wess Roberts proposed that a good role model for this kind of strong leadership was Attila the Hun—because he knew how to secure a position of advantage before making his move. Attila realised that:

- Chieftains must know when, where and with whom to take sides. Therefore, they should keep fully apprised of activities within their own nation—and within the enemy's nation.
- Chieftains who plan to fight great battles in the future do well to maintain diplomatic ties with current enemies, because today's foes can become tomorrow's comrades-in-arms.
- Because an ignored ally becomes indifferent or hostile, the best chieftains nourish even well-established relationships.[5]

Valour

On the field of battle, heroism is usually linked with selfless valour. Heroes are more concerned with the lives of others than they are with their own. This means that heroes are prepared to make sacrifices in order to save a situation or people in need of help. The metamyth or sub-text of the sacrifice theme is that 'good eventually triumphs over evil'. Not all myths, however, are remembered for their heroes' triumphs. In some myths, heroes meet tragic ends. A notable example is Tennyson's depiction of the final words of the legendary King Arthur of Camelot as he lies mortally wounded from battle:

> *The old order changeth, yielding place to new,*
> *And God fulfils himself in many ways,*
> *Lest one good custom should corrupt the world.*
> *Comfort thyself: what comfort is in me?*
> *I have lived my life, and that which I have done*
> *May He within himself make pure! but thou,*
> *If thou shouldst never see my face again,*
> *Pray for my soul.*[6]

Sacrifice

In primitive and religious mythology, sacrifice is a powerfully recurrent theme. The *Bible* abounds with examples—that of Jesus Christ, who suffered crucifixion so that God would allow believers to have eternal life; Abraham's sacrifice of his son Isaac (whose life was spared at the last minute). Classical mythology also had the recurrent theme of sacrifice. As young girls, the Amazons, a society of warrior women, were required to sacrifice one breast so that they could shoot with a bow or throw a spear more freely. In early Roman history, Horatius single-handedly defended a bridge across the Tiber River and repelled the onslaught of the Etruscan invaders. While he was doing this, he was wounded in one leg. As a result of his courageous defence of the bridge, Horatius became permanently lame.

Modern organisational myths also feature the theme of sacrifice. Organisational heroes often give something up—their time, their energy, their expertise, even their money—to help the company and its members. There are undoubtedly organisations whose mythical heroes sacrificed executive privileges like an expensive company vehicle or a paid membership of an exclusive golfing club in order to save the jobs of threatened employees. Some leaders work very long hours each day to find new ways of improving the working conditions of staff by ensuring that their budgets give priority to the acquisition and maintenance of technology that will reduce the amount of routine labour.

> Ms I. M. Noble, Head of the Accounts Department at Scrooge Investment Services, noticed that Noel Presson was doing many hours of overtime each week because the CEO, Mr Ty Twadd, would not agree to purchasing a computer with an appropriate accounting software package. Noel never complained to Ms Noble. He just got on with the tedious task of recording everything in handwritten files. Ms Noble had saved some money for an overseas holiday. She proposed to Mr Twadd that she spend her holiday money to purchase a computer for Noel's use in the company, on condition that Mr Twadd paid her back each week with the amount saved on Noel's overtime pay. Mr Twadd agreed. Noel stopped working overtime and within a few months Ms Noble had recovered all her money. She is remembered still as the manager who postponed her overseas trip for a year because the holiday money she had saved could be used to help one of her staff.

The wicked tempter

In classical mythology, the gifted musician Orpheus could not resist the temptation to look back to see if his wife Eurydice was indeed following him out of the Underworld. When he did so, he broke his agreement with the Underworld King not to look back while he was leading Eurydice back to Earth. Eurydice disappeared into the Underworld, lost forever to the heartbroken Orpheus. The *Bible*, too, has the theme of temptation in its mythology. Jesus, for instance, was tempted by the devil Satan to turn stones into bread, to leap off the top of a temple and survive, and to accept all the kingdoms of this world as long as he would worship Satan. Here 'tempt' means to 'challenge' or 'provoke' as in 'Thou shalt not tempt the Lord thy God'.[7] Satan tempted Eve, and Eve tempted Adam with the Forbidden Fruit; Mephistopheles tempted Faust with the promise of knowledge and power over others in return for his soul.

Vengeance

Revenge, or vengeance, is another occasional theme in primitive mythology. In the *Metamorphoses*, the Roman poet Ovid tells the story of a handsome young man, Narcissus, who seemed indifferent to the advances of women, including the nymph Echo, who loved him. These rejected women appealed to the god Nemesis for vengeance. Nemesis caused Narcissus to fall in love with his own reflection as he bent down to drink from a stream. Narcissus continued to watch his face in the water until he died. The *Old Testament* makes numerous references to vengeance as an attribute of God,[8] and Hera, wife of Zeus, was noted for her capacity to revenge herself upon the women her husband took as lovers.

In modern organisational mythology, revenge often appears as an offshoot of the sibling rivalry theme. It is also associated with the theme of jealousy. Characteristics like jealousy, vengefulness and succumbing to temptation are truly 'human' and natural weaknesses. Although organisational heroes should be able to rise above temptation and overcome jealous or vengeful urges, the need to 'save face' or restore credibility may cause some to counter-attack those who wrong them. The story of Saul and David demonstrates how destructive and difficult business relationships become when jealousy and revenge intervene.

Themes, archetypes, heroes and metaphors

> Saul was a very popular department manager in Wholesale Firearms & Weapons Pty Ltd. In particular, Saul was famous for his courage, innovation, initiative and resolute decision-making. He had introduced new product lines such as .22 calibre rifles with telescopic sights and tripods for heavy duty hand guns. As business in Saul's department swelled, Saul began to look for new staff. His eldest teenage son, Jonathan took on part-time work in sales on weekends and on Thursday evenings when late-night shopping was permitted. But Saul's best new recruit was David, a bright-eyed youth to whom everyone took an instant liking.
>
> David took his job very seriously. When war broke out in Mozania, a third world country, Wholesale Firearms & Weapons tendered for a contract to supply armaments to the Mozanian government. David designed a cost-efficient new lightweight automatic mortar which he named 'the slingshot'. This mortar was portable and had an effective range of 150 metres. David offered to demonstrate his new invention in Mozania. He went to the battle action zone and actually managed to kill one of the rebel guerilla chiefs, Colonel Goliath Filistyne. The chief of staff of the Mozanian Republican Forces was delighted with the new weapon and placed a huge order with Wholesale Firearms & Weapons.
>
> Pretty soon, members of Saul's department began to speak of David as Saul's successor. Saul became very resentful and jealous of David and began to look for a reason to sack him. David sensed Saul's anger towards him and voluntarily resigned from the company.

In this story, there are really two heroes, one of whom eventually becomes an anti-hero. Saul has a high profile in his company but this is eclipsed when the younger David begins to make his presence felt. Once Saul is transformed into a jealous manager, he ceases to support the talented David, whom he himself appointed. Ultimately, the result is a lose-lose outcome.

Unique themes in organisations

While we have examined some recurring and less common themes in primitive mythology and seen how these can have parallels in contemporary organisational mythologies, we are probably still tempted to ask 'Are there myths which are unique to particular organisations?'. Mostly, we think myths are unique because they are about very distinctive people or their heroic exploits, someone who is eccentrically different from any other person.

The point which needs to be made is that unique themes in organisational myths are pretty rare. Over a decade ago, a team of researchers at Cornell University attempted to uncover the rudiments of a mythology common to all organisations. These researchers noted that 'we are just beginning to understand the extent to which substantially different organisations share common cultural elements'.[9] Their observation tends to support the view that common or recurrent themes can be found in the mythologies of different organisations. So, this may be a good time for us to turn our attention to the legendary characters who first displayed the qualities of heroes in subsequent organisational myths and who, in their own way, are like thematic symbols in the myths of many organisations. Every myth has its theme, and every theme depends upon the action of some archetypal character.

Archetypes

Archetypes are the original models on which later behaviours have been patterned. In Jungian psychology, an archetype is a tendency to form primordial images or representations of a theme. According to Carl Jung, much of this happens when we dream. He suggested that:

> *The experienced investigator of the mind can . . . see the analogies between the dream pictures of modern [people] and the products of the primitive mind, its 'collective images', and its mythological motifs.*[10]

Being part of the 'collective unconscious' of our society, archetypes are like traditions which recur from generation to generation. For example, 'the hero figure is an archetype, which has existed since time immemorial.'[11]

Despite the potential richness of archetypes as keys to understanding our present world through its mythologies, it is indeed unfortunate that very little scholarship has been undertaken on archetypes. In one ingenious analysis, Barbara Bird conceptualised the Roman God Mercury as an 'entrepreneurial archetype'.[12]

The following qualities of Mercury were seen by Bird to have parallels in contemporary entrepreneurs.

> *Appetite*
> Mercury's craving to have new experiences of eating meat was like the entrepreneur's passion for independence, self-employment and control.
>
> *Vision of the possible*
> Like Mercury, modern entrepreneurs know how to use available resources to create opportunities. This reinforces the entrepreneurial credo that 'being able to use a resource is more important than owning it'.
>
> *Changing direction*
> Just as Mercury controls branching pathways, modern entrepreneurs can find branching pathways of opportunity.
>
> *Fast action*
> With his winged feet and cap of invisibility, Mercury could move quickly without detection or inhibition. Entrepreneurs, too, have the ability to act quickly on opportunities as they arise.
>
> *Networking*
> Mercury was the model of a 'good communicator'. He linked people from different places by the news he swiftly brought them. By knowing how to communicate effectively with others, entrepreneurs create for themselves access to capital, labour, information and psychological support.

Adam and Eve

There are other notable archetypes we can identify in the world of myth. For instance, Adam and Eve figure prominently as archetypes in the creation myth discussed earlier in the chapter. Both Adam and Eve were depicted as innocent and 'unashamed' of their nakedness when they were created. Later on, Eve was tempted by the serpent in the garden of Eden and ate the forbidden fruit of the tree of knowledge of good and evil. When she found this food pleasing, she gave Adam some to try. In this way, Adam and Eve lost their innocence.

The Adam and Eve story shows how archetypes can be constructed allegorically. An 'allegory' is a figurative representation of a subject under the guise of another. For example, spiritual themes can be communicated in concrete or material ways. In the Adam and Eve myth, the spiritual message might be that disobeying God, or 'sinning', will incur punishment—exclusion from Paradise. Part of the consequence of sinning is discovering the meaning of evil and learning to differentiate evil from good.

The story tells us much more. We learn about such human qualities as curiosity, susceptibility to temptation and something of the nature of relationship between woman and man.

Douglas McGregor, the well-known management scholar, also uses the archetypes of Adam and Eve to explain his 'Theory X'. He argues that people's dislike and avoidance of work parallels Adam and Eve's punishment when they were expelled from the garden of Eden and condemned to work for their livelihood.[13]

Another thinker to use Adam as an archetype was Herzberg, who developed a theory about the motivation to work. Herzberg classified human needs into two categories. Needs concerned with the Animal-Adam nature of humans were associated with the avoidance of pain which the environment can cause. Herzberg believed that a person's psychological environment is the major source of pain. The other category of needs was people's Human-Abraham nature 'which is concerned with approaching self-fulfillment or psychological growth through the accomplishment of tasks'.[14]

Organisational creation myths frequently have characters modelled on archetypes like Adam and Eve. Matching Adam's weakness and inability to be resolute is his pathetic attribution of blame to Eve when he says to God 'The woman whom thou gavest to be with me, she gave me of the tree, and I did eat'.[15] This is a clear instance of 'passing the buck' for a misdemeanour. At no point is there even a hint of nobility or heroism on the part of Adam in shielding his partner by asserting 'it was all my fault'. On the other hand, Eve frankly admits to being beguiled by the serpent. She blames no one but herself for not resisting the serpent's temptation. There will be those who are unable to withstand the forces of temptation or evil. Having succumbed, some will own up and take their medicine bravely while others will try to worm their way out with feeble excuses.

The earth mother

Another powerful archetype can be found in the Greek goddess, Demeter, whose Roman counterpart was Ceres. Demeter was the Mother Goddess of the Earth. One day while she was picking flowers, Demeter's beautiful daughter Persephone was captured and dragged into the Underworld by Hades, who had fallen in love with her. Demeter was so distraught that she neglected her godly duties of caring for the Earth. It became cold and barren. When Zeus, the king of the gods on Mount Olympus, found out what had happened, he ordered Hades to release Persephone for six months of each year to be with her mother. During these times, the Earth would become fruitful as Persephone's return to Earth signalled the beginning of the spring season. Hades agreed, on the condition that she return to the underworld for the winter, during which time Demeter mourns her daughter and the earth sleeps.

The predominant characteristics of 'Mother Earth' are her nurturing nature and her caring for her offspring. Generally, Earth is portrayed as a female and is an archetype in many primitive religions and mythologies. The Earth Mother archetype has its counterpart in organisational mythologies. For example, consider Anita Roddick's Body Shop—an international chain of stores. Commencing with just one shop in 1976, the organisation has grown to over 1100 branches in 45 countries today. Founded on the core values of 'care for the environment, concern for human rights and opposition to the exploitation of animals', the Body Shop draws heavily on the values embodied by the Earth Mother, who is inspirational, nurturing, caring and conscious of her responsibilities.

Contemporary organisations can usually identify members who fit the archetype of the nurturer, but these are not necessarily always women. Indeed, some modern female managers have felt compelled to adopt more aggressive styles in order to blend into the male-dominated cultures of their organisations. Regardless of gender, managers who are concerned with group maintenance and teambuilding among their staff usually display qualities like those of Demeter. Hers is the power of fruitfulness, generosity and instinctive creativity.

The warrior-king

Since the proper use of power is an important factor in the life of an organisation, it is only natural that there be an archetype of a power figure. In classical mythology, the most appropriate deity is Zeus whose Roman equivalent was Jupiter. Zeus was both the King of the Gods and the Ruler of the Skies. As such, he controlled the climate and elements with weapons like lightning, thunder, hail and rain. To Zeus is attributed the 'great flood' from whose consequences Deucalion and Pyrhha were spared. In contemporary organisations, the most likely counterparts of Zeus are CEOs. Their thunderbolts are their proclamations through written or spoken stories. By analogy, the visionary use of meteorological weaponry can create a positive climate within the organisation. Presumably, managers can use their power to create a warm sunny atmosphere just as they can cause their empires to be uncomfortably cold and stormy. In the latter instance, the objective may be to 'divide and conquer' the staff. King Arthur is another legendary warrior, as are Boadicea, Thor and Hercules. They defend a cause or principle against great odds, or are engaged upon some quest or search.

Dionysian revellers and a cast of thousands

For organisations of today, there are many other possible archetypes we could draw from primitive religions and mythologies. The Greek God Dionysus, for example, serves as an archetype for extraverted revellers and merrymakers. Also known as Bacchus in Roman mythology, Dionysus was associated with wine drinking and fecundity. In the Roman Republic, drunken revels became associated with the celebration of the Bacchanalia, a public festival which was banned by the Roman Senate in 186 BC. Many organisations have people modelling themselves on Dionysus. These are the 'life of the party' and see their goal as the maintenance of good morale and a positive culture in their organisations.

There are many more examples of archetypal characters that feature again and again in mythology: the sage, the healer, the hermit, the visionary, the fool, the hearthkeeper, the priestess, the imp of mischief, the crone, the student, the oracle. Any or all of these could be found in modern organisations.

The uses of archetypes

Perhaps the question you may be asking now is: 'Is all this Jungian stuff about archetypes nothing but the product of a highly vivid imagination?'.

Marc Hequet, writing about myth as a human development tool, was prompted to be even more direct:

> *Let's put the question bluntly: Under what sort of business circumstances might a CEO or a training director wake up one morning and declare, 'What we really need around here is a Jungian consultant to help our employees harmonise their conscious and unconscious minds'?*[16]

Silly as this may seem at first glance, it is exactly what is beginning to happen in some American companies. Organisational consultants like Dr Arthur Colman from Sausalito, California, are starting to argue that people want to understand their organisations more than superficially. On a one-to-one basis, consultants like Arthur Colman can help people recognise the archetypes residing in their unconscious minds. This awareness unlocks the energy from that archetype and thus becomes available in the consciousness of the person. Once this happens, people are in a position to create their life scripts for story-telling and myth-making.

Although we'll leave the topic of archetypes for the moment, we should remind ourselves that archetypes need not only be found in the literature of primitive or religious mythology. Other historical persons, even in most recent times, can serve as inspirational models for organisational communication and behaviour. We will take up this idea more fully in the following section.

Heroes

In our society, comic book characters have become heroes and role-models of uprightness, courage, honesty, faithfulness and plain old goodness. Female heroes include Modesty Blaise, Brenda Starr, Blondie Bumstead, Mary Marvel, Superwoman—even, among the young, the exuberant and independent Tank Girl. Among comic strip male heroes are the Lone Ranger, Zorro, Prince Valiant, Dick Tracy, Batman and the Phantom. Because there is so much reliance on visual imagery in cartoons and comic strips, the myths are formatted and packaged very much like condensed books or stories.

Heroic role models don't only come from comic books. From detective stories we have Agatha Christie's Miss Marple and Sara Paretsky's V.I. Warshawski. The MI5 agent 007, James Bond, created by Ian Fleming, is a hero in both books and movies. Kay Scarpetta, heroine of Patricia Cornwell's crime thrillers, uses more brain than brawn to catch her villains. Over the years, the number of such fictitious heroic role-models has increased, with the introduction of movie characters like Luke Skywalker, Indiana Jones, Dirty Harry Callahan, and Sigourney Weaver's character, Ripley, from the *Alien* trilogy.

Many heroic role-models have come from the ranks of true-life sporting personalities. Famous athletes have been perceived by their adoring fans to possess heroic qualities like persistence, bravery, determination, dedication and a willingness to work hard at training. All of these heroic characters have the potential to become role-models for members of organisations and thus to become the inspiration for characters in organisational myths.

John McEnroe always regarded Rod Laver as his idol. Boris Becker thinks Bjorn Borg was the greatest player of all time. Today's women players remember with reverence legendary champions like Margaret Court, Billie Jean King, Chris Evert, Evonne Cawley and Martina Navratilova. Highly ranked international squash players of today still remain in awe of Heather McKay, the world champion for many years, and her contemporary, Geoff Hunt.

Perhaps the heroes in financial institutions are legendary financial wizards, like Warren Buffet, just as the heroes in manufacturing companies are people who may have been originally responsible for the design of new product lines, such as Ralph Sarich or Alessi.

Can there be 'generic' heroes, then? In Ayn Rand's novel *Atlas Shrugged*, the hero was John Galt, a visionary who established a community of talented people. These gifted professionals were inspired by Galt's leadership and as a result withdrew from their society where creativity was valued no differently or no more highly than mediocrity. Galt attracted people from all walks of life—engineers, architects, builders, scientists—who could make original contributions in a community which supported originality and inventiveness.

Themes, archetypes, heroes and metaphors

Are there John Galts—latter-day Lorenzo de Medicis—who could become heroic role-models across a range of different organisations?

Our sporting heroes do have qualities which are admired by participants in other sports. Kieran Perkins, the Olympic and world swimming champion over 400, 800 and 1500 metre distances, is a universal hero not only because of his remarkable performances in the pool but also because of his gracious and unassuming manner. In all his interviews, he has never sounded boastful and has always praised the achievements of his competitors. This could equally apply to other world champions like the English Channel swimmer Susie Moroney, the cyclist Kathy Watt or the marathon runner Steve Monaghetti. All these people have universally recognised qualities that have made them legends in their time.

In organisational life, it is possible that universal heroes also exist as role-models. A freelance troubleshooter named Red Adair was typically called in by various companies to avert large-scale catastrophes. On one occasion Red Adair co-ordinated the rescue of a group of oil rig workers on a floating platform which was being destroyed by ferocious waves whipped up in a typhoon. Adair's courage was legendary. In many organisations, people spoke of someone who had acted heroically as 'having done a Red Adair'.

Fearlessness in the face of adversity or seemingly impossible odds is one trait of universal heroes. There are well-known stories of heroes who worked themselves to the point of near exhaustion in order to rescue others trapped in collapsed mine shafts or tunnels. In hospitals, surgical teams have worked through the night to save the lives of patients in critical condition. During droughts in the height of summer, bushfire brigade officers have risked their lives for days or even weeks at a time to protect private homes and community property. What has made the work of all these people even more heroically memorable is that they have not sought publicity or notoriety for their skills. They were content to apply their talents for the benefit of others in their community.

Since the industrial and technological revolution which accelerated in the nineteenth century, many famous individuals could be cited as archetypal heroes. These people are not necessarily remembered for their courage alone but also for other equally important qualities.

Part II: The organisational myth

Modern myth-makers

Thomas Watt	Invented the steam engine
Florence Nightingale	Reformed hospital nursing
Marie and Pierre Curie	Discovered radium
Louis Pasteur	Founded microbiology
Joseph Lister	First person to use antiseptics in surgery
Alexander Fleming	Discovered penicillin
Amelia Earhart	First woman to make a solo flight over the Atlantic
Amy Johnson	Record flight from England to Australia
Charles Bukowski	Unconventional poet, novelist and cult hero
Emmeline Pankhurst	Fought for women's suffrage
Thomas Alva Edison	Invented the incandescent light and the phonograph (among other things)
John Logie Baird	Demonstrated first TV transmitter
Yuri Alekseyevitch Gagarin	Made first spaceflight in Vostok 1
Dr Christian Barnard	Performed first human heart transplant
President Nelson Mandela	Fought apartheid in South Africa
Aleksandr Solzhenitsyn	Soviet novelist and 1970 Nobel Prizewinner
Martin Luther King	American civil rights leader
Sir Edmund Hillary and Sherpa guide Tensing	First people to reach the summit of Mount Everest
Thor Heyerdahl	Sailed a balsa wood raft across an ocean to demonstrate the cultural link between the Peruvians and the Polynesians.

These creative heroes possessed qualities like persistence, conscientiousness, dedication and commitment. They never gave up until they achieved their goals. Their heroism, therefore, is celebrated not only for their ultimate achievement but also for the way in which they went about their work. Both aspects have benefited humankind. As members of society today, we are reaping the rewards of the efforts of these pioneers but we are also richer for having them as role-models of the qualities we admire in our community and organisational leaders. Equivalent heroes in our organisations are not afraid to run the risk of unpopularity or censure if in the long run the things that they stand for are realised and can enhance the welfare of fellow workers.

For some people, archetypal heroes were famous military leaders. From the Greco-Roman world, there were notable generals like Macedon's Alexander the Great, Carthage's Hannibal and Rome's Julius Caesar. During the Crusades, the English King Richard the Lionheart had become a legend. Following the French Revolution, the Emperor Napoleon Bonaparte extended the territory ruled by France throughout Europe until his defeat at the Battle of Waterloo. In World War II, colourful generals from both sides included Rommel, Montgomery, Patton, Bradley and Eisenhower. All these military leaders are remembered for their strategic vision. As such, they are role-models for managers who want to be seen as visionaries tactically planning moves to create advantages for their organisations.

The hero's journey

All this brings us to the notion of 'the hero's journey'. According to Joseph Campbell, heroes periodically undertake 'journeys' where they experience a variety of trials, adventures and triumphs.[17] Typically, the hero's journey begins with a 'call' from another for help. If the call is not heeded by the hero, a second call may be sounded. This call often coincides with a significant event like losing a job or having a serious accident. On accepting the call, the hero goes through a stage of 'initiation' when the skills to undertake the journey are acquired. At this point, the hero, assesses the probability of successfully journeying alone and usually seeks out 'allies'. These can be human, technical or spiritual resources. One recurring motif in primitive mythology is that heroes can gain help from animals. The fable of Androcles and the Lion is a good example. Having removed a thorn from the lion's paw, Androcles was spared, at a later time, a mauling from the lion who recognised him.

Supported in this way, the hero commences the journey and encounters a series of 'trials' and obstacles. The 'breakthrough' eventuates when the hero surpasses all expectations to 'come through' having dealt with the trials and obstacles. The successful breakthrough then leads to a 'celebration' of the hero's triumph. Ultimately, the heroes return home. The template from which all such journeys are cut must surely be Homer's *Odyssey*. Many modern movies are based on the theme and plot of 'the hero's journey'. Typical examples include the Indiana Jones classics like *Raiders of the Lost Ark* and *Indiana Jones and the Last Crusade*, or the more ambitious *Apocalyspe Now*.

Over the years in real life, the hero's journey has characterised the exploits and adventures of prominent people such as Nelson Mandela or General Douglas Macarthur, and, in Australia, controversial figures like Lindy Chamberlain, who was finally exonerated after her trial and ordeal of being found guilty and sentenced. The hero's journey, however, is not confined to public figures. In any kind of organisation, its mythical heroes will most likely have gone through the experiences of being summoned, challenged by trials and blockages, overcoming these, being celebrated and receiving tribute, and finally marching home victorious.

In an ingenious piece of non-traditional research, three scholars used Campbell's 'Hero's Journey' as an analogy for understanding managerial high performance myths. They concluded that there were four mythical styles of managerial high performance located on a continuum ranging from the 'Journey of Intense Achievement' to the 'Journey of Collective Fulfillment'. Different kinds of transformational leaders would typically take either kind of journey. As they suggest in a specific example:

> ... whereas [General] Patton was likely on the Journey of Intense Achievement, Gandhi [India's spiritual leader] was likely on the Journey of Collective Fulfillment. Although both myths are self-authoring, the myths lead to very different experiences for the people being influenced by the myth holder. One provides for considerable freedom by encouraging individuals to develop their own personal myth, whereas the other suggests more dominance over those being influenced.[18]

The heroes in organisational myths have similar qualities to heroes on the world stage. In our organisations, we admire people who have determination to achieve the best they can for those they serve. We also have a high regard for colleagues who show courage in making decisions and who assume responsibility for those decisions even if they prove to be unwise, injudicious or harmful. Heroic managers will persist until they 'get it right' even if this means working long hours. Like the daring adventurers we have spoken of, our manager-heroes will be excited by the prospect of new challenges which may involve facing the unknown. These are the kinds of people we portray as heroes in the myths we craft, tell and listen to in our story-telling organisations.

The language of organisational myths—metaphor

The language of primitive myths is often associated with ideas and concepts that are removed from the everyday world. In Germanic mythology, *Valhalla* was the hall of the slain warriors. It was filled with *einherjar*, the souls of champions brought there by the *valkyries*, who were the personal attendants of Odin, King of the Slain. Another example is the Buddhist notion of *nirvana*. This is a state of passionless inner peace people can attain through transcendence of natural human desires. When people attain nirvana, they become free of pain, worry and the influences and pressures of the external world.

In our daily dealings we speak in a curious mixture of cliché and metaphor, repeating 'sound bites' from movies and commercials and TV shows. Jargon from our occupations is also spread around. So, mums with headaches 'soldier on' with Codral. Kylie Minogue believes in sticking with 'the devil you know'. This hybrid nature of our everyday language suggests that the use of analogy and metaphor is not confined exclusively to communication in our workplaces. We do, however, tend to tailor the kind of language we use to the particular audience we are engaging.

A team leader, for example, may resort to military metaphor in order to unite 'the troops' for a common strategic objective. In Shakespeare's play, *Henry V*, the English king's exhortation to his forces on the eve of the Battle of Agincourt is a model for a passionate pep talk:

We few, we happy few, we band of brothers;
For he to-day that sheds his blood with me
Shall be my brother; be he ne'er so vile,
This day shall gentle his condition;
And gentlemen in England now a-bed
Shall think themselves accurs'd they were not here.[19]

Alternatively, a newly recruited member of staff may be welcomed into the 'family' by the managing director. Much of our daily talk can be fairly prosaic, lacking colour and richness because our focus is substantially on what we see as matters-of-fact. However, when we create or rescript our myths to give life to the culture of our workplaces, our crafting tends to be creative, drawing on a wealth of imagery and figurative devices such as simile and metaphor. The myth-as-work-of-art is thus likely to be preserved and remembered as something striking and attention-catching by other sharers in the story network and culture.

Modern organisational myths also have a language characterised by images and metaphors not literally associated with the normal life and culture of the organisation. These metaphors, however, carry connotations which enable people to view their organisations differently—through new ways of interpreting the communication and relationships which take place between people. We all know there is an inextricable relationship between language and thinking. Our thinking is shaped by the language we use. Being aware of the metaphors and images people draw on when telling their stories and myths is a vital step to understanding the meaning of events, human behaviour and communication in organisations.

The language of family

One popular way of describing some modern organisations is by using *family language*. For example, we often hear references to the *parent company*, so we think of subsidiary companies as the children of the larger entity. Within the organisation, we may also hear references to the CEO or the Chairman of the Board as *the old man at the top*. It is an image of a parent or guardian wisely (or dictatorially) protecting the family. Sometimes, the children can get out of line or decide that they can't take it any more. This is when they *spit the dummy*.

The notion of 'family' connotes 'belonging', in the way that a relative belongs to a group bonded by kinship. Organisations that see themselves as families may differ in the way that conventional families do—large organisations with a strong team culture may be likened to extended families, in contrast to small, family-owned businesses, which may even literally be nuclear families. Of course, there is also a negative side to belonging to a family. Patriarchal and paternalist practices such as 'nepotism' can damage relationships within the family by creating rifts and factional liaisons based on the internal poilitics of the family system.

Family metaphors have been applied specifically to certain organisations. For example, a great national institution such as the Australian Broadcasting Commission (ABC) also has the name of *Aunty ABC*. Relatively speaking, therefore, the ABC is portrayed as a matriarch. Closely linked with family language is proprietorial language. People who use proprietorial language typically use expressions like *investment in people* and *the stakeholders*.

The language of physiology

In Chapter 2 organisations were likened to living bodies. The Catholic Church has been the 'body' of Christ since the early middle ages, so this is a familiar metaphor.

Some organisations have adopted a language of human physiology. People in companies where morale is low say things like the *organisation has lost heart* or *the CEO lacks guts*. Managers have their *finger on the pulse* of the organisation or they have *tunnel vision*. When the organisation's various departments are not perceived to be working co-operatively or interdependently, *the left hand does not know what the right hand is doing*.

Hands are also associated with the practicalities of work. Managers who are prepared to fill in and do the work of absent staff are *not afraid of getting their hands dirty*—they are *hands-on managers*. Gerard Egan often describes communication as the *lifeblood of the system*. Many of us have also heard of organisations cleared of allegations or charges of impropriety or illegality as having been given *a clean bill of health*. US President Bill Clinton's 1994 crusade for reforming the US health insurance system, which was eventually abandoned by Democrats in the Senate, provoked the following headline from a Washington correspondent: 'Health Reform Collapse Emasculates Clinton'.

The image of an organisation as a healthy body connotes the ideas of unity and interdependence. Since bodies require regular exercise and a balanced diet for proper maintenance, organisations-as-bodies need nurturing and periodical workouts. Sensitive and wise CEOs know when it is time to begin this process of renewal by resting its parts, by giving it relevant training or by introducing a new 'vitamin' in the daily diet of information, learning and incentives. One common practice is to take the organisation, or parts of it, off-site for a day or two to a resort environment where the corporate body can be refreshed before returning to regular duties.

Metaphors from the natural world

The language of the natural world has also made its mark on organisational communication. The metaphors are partly geological but also derive from vivid images of terrain and weather. Gung-ho managers, for instance, often want to show their staff that they are not out of touch and can still do the work their staff are required to do. So, they prove to their staff that they can *work at the coal face*. When managers make decisions in which their staff do not have confidence, they are on *shaky ground*. Sometimes executives have to face an *avalanche of questions* from members of the press.

The language of the natural world is a rich source of metaphors for mythologising and story-telling in organisations. Frequently we note that some organisations are at the leading (or cutting) edge whereas less successful companies are experiencing *a financial drought*. Even managers who have not been directly responsible for some mishap soon learn that *some of the dirt will stick*.

It's all in the game

Many of the metaphors used in organisational myths are action-oriented. Action is often associated with sport. The language of sport has significantly influenced communication and story-telling in organisations. Managers may ask project co-ordinators about the *state of play*, or suggest that it is time to *lift their game*. Organisational strategists and planners like *the game plan* or *it's a new ball game*.

Sports language has two predominant themes. One is the theme of winning and the other is one of team-building. Both themes have relevance and currency in today's organisations. Associated with the theme of winning are expressions like *pipped at the post*, *not giving the game away* and, of course, *scoring a win*. Someone in control of the game may *shift the goalposts*, or the game might not be contested on a *level playing field*. When managers surmount such obstacles, they do so because of some *masterstroke*. Members of the winning team are *the key players*. Key players are those who *choose, build, coach, lead and manage* the team.

The language of sport is not the only source of action-oriented metaphors for myths in the story-telling organisation. Seafaring metaphors and metaphors about automobiles form an integral part of the language of travel. Some of the more common images in seafaring language relate to leaders who *steer the ship* so that she can *stay on an even keel*. Decisions are made by leaders *at the helm* who may occasionally need to *chart a middle course*.

Just as leaders in seafaring language are construed as ships' captains, in automobile language the leaders are the car drivers and the car is typically a task or project. Thus, managers are described as *holding the wheel*. It is also fashionable to ask who is *driving the project*. On occasions, a manager may want to speed up or slow down the progress of the project by asking the project team to *put on the accelerator or brake pedal*.

Action-oriented metaphors, and particularly the images deriving from the world of sport, are probably among the most commonly used by professionals in today's organisations. The effect of their use is largely dependent on the accompanying attitude. For example, those who believe that what is important is not necessarily winning but 'how you play the game' are likely to support a team culture in their organisation. Those who live for their sport and take the game with deadly seriousness may not be satisfied until the opposition is crushed and humiliated in total defeat. In these circumstances, the 'sporting events' in the organisation may degenerate into political opportunism where contending parties seek to obtain advantage through intrigue and shadow side activity.

Military language

Action is also closely connected to military language and metaphors. The theme of winning is central to military language and is evidenced in expressions like *victorious, triumphant* or just *winning*. We use terms like *the front line of management*. It is common in some organisations to refer familiarly to employees as *the troops*. The word *officer* to designate specific positions has a militaristic ring to it. While the CEO can be seen as a general marshalling the organisation's forces, members of the organisation may wonder what the general's *plan of attack* will be. Will the old war horse require us to *soldier on*? Are *the big guns* going to be brought out?

Military metaphors tend to be used by and associated with the language of senior executives, such as CEOs. Famous generals and military leaders—Alexander, Hannibal, Julius Caesar, Montgomery, Patton or De Gaulle, for example—can serve as role models for people in positions of power within their organisations. Similarly, employees may come to regard their managers in terms of undesirable role models of military leadership. It is not uncommon to hear of some tyrannical manager being referred to as Ghengis Khan or Hitler. This role model-based imagery can easily be elaborated into more complex metaphor-stories.

Jargon and officialese

The language of bureaucracy, sometimes termed officialese, is perhaps best known for its euphemisms. Below are a few examples of officialese with the literal meaning given in brackets:

- downsizing (terminating the employment of some staff)
- rightsizing (reducing the number of staff in parts of the organisation)
- financial streamlining procedures (budget cuts)
- fringe benefit (taxation the executive can avoid)
- profit before tax (loss)
- supplementary statistical information (padding).

Legal jargon gives a formal air to organisational proceedings. In conflicts between employees and employers, for instance, reference may be made to *the parties in dispute* or to *the matter to be resolved*. Even in everyday conversations, people use terms like *the case in point* and *the issue in question*.

Art, religion and prophesy

The myths and stories told in many organisations use metaphors drawn from the fine arts. Typical images from the visual arts include phrases like the *big picture*, *painting (or sketching) a scenario* and *creating a vision*. Metaphors from the language of music generally refer to the musical equivalent of the big picture—the orchestra. Thus, we have the examples of a *harmonious organisation* or *a performance which sets new standards*. The orchestra is a convenient symbol for a successful work team because it is the collaborative synergy of its members that results in a great performance.

Visual art metaphors are closely related to prophetic language which is characterised by phrases like *visionary* or *prophet of doom*. Prophetic metaphors are probably a subset of religious metaphors. Many religious metaphors have become part of everyday discourse. For example, we often hear expressions such as *angel of mercy*, *I'll sing your praises* or *the devil you know*. In some cases, people allude to particular Biblical characters in the metaphors they use—a *doubting Thomas* or a *Jeremiah*. We talk about people having the *wisdom of Solomon*, the *patience of Job* or the *strength of Samson*. Biblical places and events also occur metaphorically in organisational myths—expressions like going *into the lion's den*, having *a cross to bear* or *I wash my hands of it* (referring to Pontius Pilate's words before pronouncing sentence on Jesus Christ).

Symbols

The power of symbols within organisational myth can be profound. Just as Christianity is represented succinctly but mystically by the Cross, just as the Holy Grail instantly recalls the quests of chivalrous knights, symbols can be used potently within organisational myths.

> There is a story about a corporation whose CEO had tried every management fad he could think of to boost his comapny's ailing performance. Finally, having decided that as a last desperate measure he would ask his employees what they thought he should do, he had his office door removed at night and hung from wires in the head office foyer. He sent out a memo to all employees that they were free to attend any meeting at all held anywhere in the company, and that they were always welcome to go and speak with him. The door remains hanging in the foyer of a now-successful company as a powerful symbol of openness.

> In another organisation, the CEO set up a traffic light outside his office door. When the light was red, he was unavailable, and people would enter at their peril. The orange light signalled that people should wait briefly until the light changed to green, when it was safe to go in. The overall effect of this was a company in which employees felt that the CEO had an open door only when it suited him. The traffic light symbolised control, and a policing of access to the chief, just as the hanging door in the previous company implied empowerment of employees.

All these various categories and types of metaphor have the potential to influence the perception that people have of organisational myths and stories. Many of us would recognise the type of people about whom myths are created but we probably have not given much thought to this in our own organisations. Until now we probably haven't thought much about organisations being held together by stories and myths. Ask yourself now: 'How does what I have read and thought about so far help me understand and lead my organisation more effectively than in the past? Do I know my organisation's dominant stories and myths? Does this knowledge give me a big picture of the life and culture of my organisation? Where do I go from here?'

Summary

In this chapter, we have journeyed deeper into the world of organisational myths. We have explored common and recurrent themes in primitive mythology and seen how these have parallels in the story-telling organisation. As well, we have noted that on occasions there may be myths whose themes are specific to certain organisations. Next, we have identified some archetypes in organisational myths. We have found that these could serve as role-models for our own story-telling, communication and actions. Some of these archetypes are clearly recognisable legendary heroes. The plots of many contemporary organisational myths, however, are woven around true-life characters with attributes modelled on those of historical archetypes. Myths, as we have seen, put us in the picture about life in our organisations. In this way, we are enabled to understand more profoundly and come to terms with the culture of our organisations. This is the theme we will develop more fully in Part III.

building the story-telling organisation

5

creating and changing organisational culture

To know the world, one must construct it.
Cesare Pavese

We are now entering the fascinating world of organisational culture. In this chapter we'll find out how organisations create and develop their cultures through myths and story-telling. We'll ask what the 'shadow side' is and how we can understand and manage it in our working lives. Because we are all change agents of one kind or another, we'll explore ways of bringing about necessary changes to our organisations and their cultures through story-telling. Finally, we'll consider ways of building a positive, open, healthy story-telling culture in our own organisations.

What is organisational culture?

According to Peters and Waterman,

> ... *stories, myths and legends appear to be very important, because they convey the organisation's shared values, or culture.*[1]

They note that those companies they identified as 'excellent' had obvious shared values and rich mythologies. Organisations whose members share values like quality service, faultless products, innovation, initiative, enterprise, open communication and trust are bound to be successful. By contrast, organisations whose culture is based on 'the way we do things around here' are likely to be inward-looking and resistant to fresh ideas from the external environment.

Climate and culture

Some people tend to relate an organisation's culture to its structure. When this happens, culture may be confused with 'climate'. Using a meteorological analogy, we can explain 'organisational climate' as the 'weather pattern' or 'atmosphere' of that organisation. The story-telling organisation's atmosphere is typically conducive to open communication and frequent contact among members. In many large bureaucracies, on the other hand, open communication is more difficult because of the inaccessibility of certain individuals to the entire membership of the organisation. There the atmosphere can be 'chilling' and forbidding.

There is some connection between the culture and climate of organisations since 'culture informs climate in a number of important ways, most notably through the influence of organisational leadership'.[2] Gerald Goldhaber explained the distinction between organisational climate and culture like this:

> [C]limate is often short term and may depend upon current management of an organisation, but culture is usually long term, rooted in deeply held values, and often very hard to change.[3]

Climate may thus be thought of as a measure of whether the work expectations of members in organisations are being met, whereas culture refers to the nature of those expectations.

Values and artefacts

The values, attitudes and beliefs within an organisation are determinants of observable behaviours which form an integral part of the organisation's overt culture. Complementing values, attitudes and beliefs are the 'artefacts' of organisational culture. Stories and myths are artefacts. So are rituals, ceremonies, norms, the physical environment and management practices. Both values and artefacts form part of the 'visible' or overt culture of organisations and can thus be related to dimensions of organisational climate. Underlying the visible culture are basic assumptions and understandings which people have about the ways their organisations operate.[4] These assumptions are generally located deep in the unconscious mind and are like people's established perceptions of their organisation's rules. Being part of people's unconscious, basic assumptions form part of the 'invisible culture' of organisations. Sackmann saw basic assumptions as the 'hidden components' of organisational culture, much like the mass below the tip of an iceberg.[5]

Most people think of culture associated with groups of people who make up organisations. In other words, organisational culture is represented by the collective logic and mythology of a system's entire membership. The temptation to see an organisation's culture as the uniform sum or average of its members' values, beliefs and practices is fairly strong. Stipulating that everyone in the system subscribes to a set of shared values, attitudes, beliefs, norms and artefacts and that these represent exactly how everyone in the organisation thinks and feels is a neat solution to complexity. When people succumb to this temptation, they assume that the actual values of individual members are the same as the values they think all members of the organisation should hold.

This may be true of some organisations but simplistic equations of this kind can lead to very inaccurate interpretations of an organisation's culture. Members of an organisation do not invariably think the same way, hold the same values, believe the same things or communicate and act identically. Shared values, beliefs and practices, however, result in what we commonly term the 'culture' of the system.

Geert Hofstede argues that

> ... *culture is not a characteristic of individuals; it encompasses a number of people who were conditioned by the same education and life experience.*[6]

Hofstede regards life in organisations as the microcosmic equivalent of particular national cultures.

Cross-cultural influences

In today's world, organisational cultures are beginning to be influenced by practices in other national cultures. During the 1980s, American and Australian organisations were influenced by Japanese 'quality control circles'. The Japanese learned this technique from W. Edward Deming, an American. 'Quality circles' consist of small groups of workers who meet regularly to solve organisational problems. These may stem from inefficient production methods, low morale among employees, poor team-work and the need to help staff develop production skills.

An exploration of cross-cultural influences on an organisation can be found in the work of William Ouchi. His ideal organisation was based on a mixture of the strengths of both traditional American and Japanese systems. The American strengths of quick decision-making, risk-taking, innovative management and respect for the independence of individual staff members would be complemented by Japanese strengths in human resource management, including a concern for the welfare of employees. Ouchi suggested that this combination of cultural values would be found in what he called a 'Theory Z organisation'.[7]

Dimensions of organisational culture

From an empirical investigation of 40 independent nations, Hofstede identified four dimensions of culture:

- power distance
- uncertainty avoidance
- individualism–collectivism
- masculinity–femininity.

Power distance refers to the degree to which a society believes power in organisations is distributed unequally. The values of powerful as well as less powerful members of society indicate the power distance in systems.

Uncertainty avoidance, the second dimension, signals the extent to which a society is threatened by uncertain or ambiguous situations. Common strategies for uncertainty avoidance in organisations might include making formal rules, forbidding ideas or behaviours that are contrary to 'the company way' and believing in absolute truths, particularly regarding the attainment of expertise. Hofstede asserts that in societies where uncertainty avoidance is high, people tend to develop the motivation to work hard.

Complementing uncertainty avoidance is *individualism–collectivism*. Members of individualistic societies tend to centre their lives on themselves and their immediate families. By contrast, in collectivist societies both 'in-groups' and 'out-groups' form. In-groups like families or organisations are expected to look after their members in exchange for their loyalty. One simple way of distinguishing individualism from collectivism is to associate 'I' thinking with individualism and 'we' thinking with collectivism.

The fourth dimension is *masculinity–femininity*. Some societies are characterised by so-called 'masculine' values like acquiring money and material possessions, whereas members of societies whose values are predominantly 'feminine' more typically care for other people and seek 'quality of life'. While Hofstede sees 'culture' as a characteristic of societies rather than of individuals, he is quick to point out that not everyone in a nation necessarily holds the values attributed to that nation's culture.

The role of story-telling

Story-telling is the process of communicating, revitalising and, if necessary, changing the culture of organisations by relating individual and corporate values. Some of the most powerful story-tellers are the charismatic leaders in organisations. These people may have more influence than other members in shaping the culture of their organisations. Nevertheless, the entire collection of members' stories is needed to piece together the mosaic of an organisation's true culture. This may be quite difficult as people are not always honest in their story-telling. How often have we thought people were saying what they thought others wanted to hear rather than what they actually believed?

The way in which stories are communicated can have a powerful effect on the organisation's culture. Harry Irwin and Elizabeth More have identified seven myths about communication, which serve to remind us that language alone does not shape an organisation's culture. Among these is the 'culture myth'—that the main or only barrier to communication is spoken or written language. In fact, the cultural differences between people within organisations can be numerous. Apart from differences in the expression of emotions facially, vocally and through gestures, there are 'cultural' differences

> ... between men and women, between age groups, between masculine and feminine cultures and backgrounds ... In the same way, there are cultural differences between occupations and even whole corporations. [8]

Workplace culture, therefore, can be complex and difficult to interpret. Organisations are naturally 'messy' because there is usually a covert or 'shadow side' complementing the overt culture. Much of what happens in the shadow side is either unpredictable or undiscussable and we can rarely be certain we have the full or true story. We will return to the shadow side later in this chapter. At this point, we need to understand that 'culture' is not something one gets a feel for merely by referring to corporate mission statements, strategic plans, annual reports or the minutes of annual general meetings.

Organisational culture types

There are at least four types of value-based cultures common to different organisations. These are:

- the 'way we do it around here' culture
- the 'she'll be right' culture
- the 'don't rock the boat' culture
- the 'top gun' culture.

'The way we do it round here'

We have already alluded to 'the way we do it around here' culture. The chief assumption made in this type of organisational culture is that best practice is company practice. Managers who think like this are often people who have been employed by the one organisation for many years. Indeed, some of the most myopic managers have only ever worked in one organisation or one industry. These managers are also quick to point out that their years of experience in the one type of industry gives them the realistic know-how which young upstart visionaries could never have. Generally, 'the way we do it around here' managers are intolerant of new ideas or change to the culture of their organisations.

'She'll be right'

The 'she'll be right' culture and the 'don't rock the boat' cultures are offshoots of 'the way we do it around here'. In organisations with a 'she'll be right' culture, little change occurs because the predominant work ethic is essentially a laid back one. No one makes a concerted effort to implement new ideas or procedures. Any outcome will be satisfactory, so let's 'take it easy' and 'let's not burst our boilers'. Until recently, much of the Australian workforce was perceived by overseas counterparts as part of a national 'she'll be right' culture. People who work in 'she'll be right' organisations aren't very fussed about what happens as long as they aren't required to make any greater effort than they are at the moment. If there's a way they can do better for themselves, especially if that means no corresponding increase in productivity, they will probably find it.

'Don't rock the boat'

In organisations with a 'don't rock the boat' culture, employees are not indifferent to change but will vigorously resist it. This is because the organisation has become a 'comfort zone' for its members. They feel good about their roles and attendant responsibilities since they continue to be noticed and applauded for their repetitious and unvarying performance of tasks.

Are there organisations where this is unavoidable? What opportunities for initiative or innovation exist in bureaucracies which follow very strict procedures for the issue of passports, drivers' licences, certificates of births, marriages and deaths, or for the deposit or withdrawal of money from bank accounts? If nothing else, there is always room to improve customer service or communication. Employees should not have to wait for instructions or company policy on 'how to do it'. Although workers may not have the power to change official documentary requirements, there is nothing to stop them from devising ways of minimising red tape.

Part III: Building the story-telling organisation

> For many years customers at most bank branches resented waiting in lines that formed in front of particular tellers. In some lines customers seemed to make their transactions more quickly than in other queues. There was no way of knowing if someone before you had two or three lengthy transactions while others only had one simple query. If you were lucky you might only need to wait 5 minutes to be served. Often, however, people might have to wait through their lunch hour to be finally served.
>
> At Forward Bank's city branch, Lionel Stopshuvvers, the accountant, noticed what was going on and made a number of suggestions to his manager, Col Laborator. These included increasing the number of tellers on duty at lunchtimes and correspondingly reducing the number in the early and late hours of business, roping off a section where customers would wait in line for the next available teller, and devising a light and audio-signal system to indicate that a teller was free to serve the next customer. Col was impressed with Lionel's suggestions and decided to put them to the test.
>
> The new procedures worked beautifully. Business doubled as customers left other banks to join Forward Bank's city branch. Col notified his superiors at head office. Before long, all branches of Forward Bank were following Lionel's suggestions. Col was soon promoted to a managership in the international division. Lionel took a branch managership. The tellers felt relieved in that they were not constantly dealing with frustrated or angry customers. And the customers were now able to get through their banking business quickly. This was a win-win solution for everybody—due to an enterprising employee not slavishly following procedures which were far from perfect.

'Top gun'

In contrast to the three kinds of organisational culture we have just examined, the 'top gun' culture is characterised by a mission and accompanying values which give the message 'we want to stay the best'. Members of 'top gun' organisations are not complacent about their current successes. They remain alert for any opportunity coming their way. When those opportunities do come, 'top gun' organisations seize them. 'Top gun' organisations welcome change if there is any further possibility of implementing the values of the system—there is always room for improvement. Unlike the other three kinds of organisations, 'top gunners' will never rest on their laurels.

Creating and changing organisational culture

Australia Post is an example of an organisation which changed from a 'she'll be right' to a 'top gun' culture.

Until the mid-1980s, Australian post offices and telephone services were under the control of the Commonwealth Government Department of the Post Master General (PMG). At post offices you bought stamps or aerogrammes, and posted or collected parcels and letters. Post offices, in fact, ran exactly as they had been operating for decades. Having no competition, post offices offered no reliable additional services like express mail. Even the services that were provided were erratic.

As a result of a restructuring of government services, the PMG split into two statutory authorities: Telecom and Australia Post. The two new organisations were entrusted with a mission to be entrepreneurial to the point where they would not be dependent on funding drawn from federal taxes.

In the years that followed, Australian post offices developed a new logo and the offices were refurbished in modern decor. New services, such as payment of public utilities accounts by credit card, were introduced. In competition with established companies, Australia Post successfully commenced courier services. Sales extended to include a range of different sized postpaks, express post envelopes, self-adhesive stamps, press-seal envelopes and a range of greeting cards.

Australia Post was now actually making money. The old PMG had operated at a financial loss, largely because its *modus operandi* was inefficient and inflexible. With new streamlined procedures, Australia Post soon earned the reputation of a quality service provider. The change to a 'top gun' culture was also evident in customer service at post offices. Postal workers also began to dress more smartly, giving the impression of being professionals. Customers were greeted with courteous offers of assistance. All in all, the transformation of postal services from the PMG to Australia Post is a clear success story.

At first the changeover wasn't easy. Many postal workers continued to operate as though nothing was different. Even with staff development and training for their new roles, it took a few years before the changes were seen by the public to be working successfully. Nowadays, it is not surprising to find some new idea being trialled at post offices. People have come to expect innovation in organisations with a 'top gun' culture. There was a parallel cultural shift in Telecom, and competition from a new company, Optus, resulted in still further improvements.

Two extreme side-effects of working in a 'top gun' organisation are stress and burnout. Terrence Deal and Alan Kennedy identified four types of corporate culture; one of them, the 'tough-guy macho' culture, was seen as characterising many of today's successful organisations.[9] Stress is often caused by competition among an organisation's members. The 'tough-guy macho' culture is highly individualistic and people work at breakneck paces demanded by success and to impress their superiors. The physical consequences of stress and burnout can be very serious, often leading to premature retirement for health reasons. Although 'top gun' organisations with a 'tough-guy macho' emphasis are often successful because key players are prepared to work hard and take risks, their deficiencies include a lack of co-operation and interdependence among members, short-term goals and a tendency towards 'superstitious behaviour' such as repeatedly making the sign of the cross before giving a new presentation at some board meeting.

Cultural indicators

There are several indicators of the nature of an organisation's culture. Pacanowsky and O'Donnell-Trujillo have listed the following:

> *Relevant constructs*
> Constructs signal how members of an organisation structure their experiences. A 'tutorial' is a construct associated with educational organisations; a 'meeting in chambers' is a construct associated with the legal profession.
>
> *A system of facts*
> Facts are used to explain the way the organisation operates. The facts make up the 'social knowledge' of the organisation. For example, it may be a fact that there are five departments in the organisation.
>
> *Practices*
> Members engage in practices to get the job done—for example, forming working parties or creating teams.
>
> *Vocabulary*
> Vocabulary refers to the language that is organisation- or profession-specific and that can indicate an organisation's constructs, facts and practices. In hospitals surgery is referred to as a 'procedure'. The word would mean different things for external consultants recruiting executive staff, or for naval personnel.

> *Metaphors*
> Metaphors are used by employees to construct meanings about their organisations. The nautical metaphor of 'taking something on board' implies an analogy between the organisation and a ship.
> *Stories*
> An organisation's values can be communicated and interpreted through stories.
> *Rituals and rites*
> Annual performance reviews, monthly board meetings, or interdepartmental sporting competitions at lunchtimes are all rituals or rites with meaning to the organisation.[10]

All seven of the above indicators can be said to be complementary components of the story-telling organisation. Stories are a part of this list; language, ritual and metaphor are essential elements of myth-making. As we have already seen, metaphors often determine the vocabulary of organisational myths which in turn create facts that underlie practices and rituals in systems. Therefore, let us examine more closely how myths and story-telling can influence an organisation's culture.

Building a culture with myth and story

We noted earlier that myths and stories are the source of an organisation's realities, including any changes to the system. Jeanie Daniel Duck, Vice President in the Chicago office of the Boston Consulting Group, noted that managing change was like balancing a mobile. She elaborated on this metaphor by stating that

> *. . . managing change means managing the conversation between the people leading the change effort and those who are expected to implement the new strategies, managing the organisational context in which change can occur, and managing the emotional connections that are essential for any transformation.*[11]

Part III: Building the story-telling organisation

The important thing to note here is the link between managing change and managing communication. Since a great deal of story-telling in organisations occurs through everyday conversations between members, any changes in the culture of the organisation are most probably attributable to powerful and persuasive stories. Some of these stories are bound to occasion emotional reactions among the story-listeners. When these emotional reactions get out of hand and go unchecked, a covert or 'shadow side' culture begins to develop in the organisation.

Subcultures

Story-telling, therefore, can either strengthen or weaken the interdependency of an organisation's members. A 'shadow side' may preclude some members from hearing stories, or at least certain versions in an organisation's mythology. This kind of selective story-telling may result in divisions among staff and in the evolution of subcultures within the system.

Subcultures tend to develop their own mini-mythologies. Jensen and Chilberg suggested that any small group with its own subculture is like 'a fish in the waters of its organisational culture'.[12] Groups whose subcultures are consistent with the corporate culture are usually part of an open communication and story-telling system. The myths of the organisation also influence the thinking and performance of people in distinct groups like departments or sections. When groups begin to think of themselves as separate entities and ignore what is happening in the rest of the organisation, the group's story-telling and mythologies can deviate considerably from the pervasive myths of the entire system. The story of Emma Maverick is a good example.

The greatest show on earth

When Willem Power decided to restructure his division, he created four new departments. Previously, the division had a very loose structure and the lines of reporting were not clear. In Willem's new structure, the four department heads were entrusted with leadership in planning, productivity, quality assurance and staff development relating to their areas of responsibility. Emma Maverick became head of the marketing and public relations department. Of the 40 staff in Willem's division, five took up Emma's open invitation to join her department. Of the rest of the staff, 20 identified with the sales department, eight with the production department and seven with the information systems department.

Being very enthusiastic, Emma gave her staff a 'pep talk' in which she emphasised that her team should regard itself as the sole expert group in the division on any marketing or public relations matters. In very broad terms, Emma communicated her vision and strategic goals to her team. She wasn't aware, however, that her counterpart in sales, Jimmy Greenback, was giving an almost identical speech to his sales team. In the looser former structure of the division, sales, marketing and public relations had come under one roof. Staff who were formerly multiskilled were now being separated in different departments whose functions overlapped.

Perhaps the most distressing outcome of the restructure was the perception by many of the division's members that Emma's team saw itself as the elite team in the division. She seemed to be projecting the image that her team could do what no other team could, despite the fact that many members of the sales department were as capable of carrying out the work as anyone in marketing and public relations. Pretty soon Emma's department acquired the nickname of 'The Greatest Show on Earth'. And myths began to develop about Emma and her team.

In one popular myth, Emma was described as a female reincarnation of the former world champion heavyweight boxer, Muhammad Ali, whose famous boast was 'I am the greatest!' Although Emma was noticeably committed and very industrious, the characteristics and motives staff in other departments associated with her were vanity, glory-seeking, empire building and self-aggrandisement. Members of 'The Greatest Show on Earth' were similarly regarded as self-styled 'high fliers' in the marketing and public relations trapeze act.

Emma's staff did not know these stories were circulating about them. Within their own team, Emma became a heroic archetype. She was seen as a hardworking leader who was always prepared to support the initiatives of any of her team. They saw her as one of the most loyal and constructive contributors to the strategic goals of the division. In the space of a few months, marketing and public relations, insulated from the rest of the division, developed its own mythology, while the other staff in the division generated a very different set of stories about Emma's team.

Emma's intentions were laudable. She just lost sight of the reality that the organisations that work best don't consist of soloists. The orchestra must harmonise and stick to a common rhythm.

Story-telling as a form of communication enables an organisation's members to 'get in touch' with all that is happening in the system's culture. When story-telling becomes confined to only part of the system, the opportunity to bind staff and create a climate for sharing the organisation's culture is severely impeded. Subsystems which operate independently of other parts of the organisation tend to inject an element of unproven speculation about their contribution to the whole system. In Emma's case, speculation about her department led to negative perceptions which created unnecessary divisions between her team and the rest of the division's staff.

Fantasy themes

Organisational culture is especially influenced by story-telling through the dynamic sharing of 'group fantasies'. According to Ernest G. Bormann, in a task-oriented meeting someone may

> ... *use dramatic imagery, wordplay, or more often tell a story in which characters enact a dramatic scenario in some other place or time than the here-and-now of the unfolding group experience.*[13]

Gradually, other people at the meeting will become involved as co-producers of the story and participate in the drama. Emotions are likely to surface, tensions may be released, and the mood of the meeting may change as participants focus directly on the dramatised story.

Fantasy-sharing often also occurs in the informal conversations among an organisation's members. Through framing stories around shared fantasies, people can reduce their uncertainties and fears about the future. For example:

○ Wouldn't it be fantastic if we could hold a retreat tomorrow with our stockholders and relax them about our proposal for a merger with Techsound Industries? We could put on a demonstration of both companies'

Creating and changing organisational culture

technical resources to prove that we'll be twice as competitive on the market. Here's what we could do . . .
- Let's imagine we're in the boss's office selling our investment plan. First, we'd try to get him to think it's all his idea by saying it was too original a scheme for any ordinary person to dream up. Only someone with his foresight could have done it. Then we'll move in with the facts and figures . . .
- One day I'm going to give that saucy customer a fat lip. Just one more complaint and I'd let him have it. What I'd really like to do is to pick him up by the shirt collar and chuck him out of the store . . .

The 'fantasy themes' above relate to a future time or different place from the present realities confronting the story-tellers. Many of the classical myths mentioned so far have fantasy themes that can provide us with illuminating insights into how we can address problems in our everyday lives. Like daydreaming, sharing fantasy themes can be very motivating—even to the point of finding solutions to personal or organisational problems.

One outcome of fantasy-sharing is the 'inside' or 'private' joke which members of a story-telling group may recall from time to time. Through the retelling of private jokes story-tellers and story-listeners can develop strong ties of friendship and loyalty to each other. Private jokes often bring about the creation of 'fantasy types'—recurring scripts in the culture of an organisation.

Some 'fantasy types' which, with different characters and settings, may be found across many organisational cultures are:

- Gosh, the boss is actually human!
- The company will look after us all when the going gets tough.
- Anyone in this organisation can make it to the top.
- We're doing so well nobody will ever downsize our section.
- As long as I keep doing a good job, I'll be appreciated/recognised for it.
- My criticisms are for the company's good—I'm sure my manager knows.

As we can see, fantasy types characteristically contain an expectation, hope or desire for the fulfilment of a group's wishes. In our shared fantasies we want or expect our superiors to be just and fair. We also look for reassurance about the security of our jobs or about career path opportunities. When our hopes, expectations or needs are dashed or thwarted in some way, we are likely to develop negative fantasy types where our heightened emotions can be expressed without threat to us. In these situations, we do not so much wish something good for ourselves, rather, we fantasise about the undoing of persons or events capable of harming or disadvantaging us. For example:

- Just you wait! Old Marble Head will fall flat on his face before long.
- My boss will be sorry she rated my current performance so low. When my new idea is approved by the vice-president, she will look a real fool for not supporting me.
- Okay, suggestions to improve our advertising strategy have been knocked back again by Skin Flint. Won't his face be red when he finds out that most of our competitors have gone the way we are suggesting and that their sales have increased enormously as a result?

People use negative fantasy types to defend themselves against things that are likely to happen by fantasising about things they would enjoy seeing come about. The wish-fulfilment themes underlying negative fantasy types often include retribution, revenge, humiliation, failure and even destruction. By using these themes, people try to deflect harm directed to themselves and imagine the perpetrators becoming the victims. Negative fantasy types thus enable people to release tensions and to feel good about themselves.

We have a fairly good idea now of how stories can contribute to an organisation's culture. As we noted earlier in this section, through story-telling we can change the culture of the systems in which we operate.

Managing change through story-telling

Organisations cannot survive without change. Many organisations that resist change rapidly become 'out of date' and gradually move to a point of self-destruction. Health and growth in organisations depends upon renewal and change. Moreover, organisations cannot afford to remain complacent once they have been identified as 'successful'. When, in 1982, Peters and Waterman published *In Search Of Excellence*, a number of companies were declared to be outstanding on eight criteria, such as staying 'close to the customer' or having 'a bias for action'. Five years down the track over two-thirds of these companies fell off their pedestals. Why? In most cases, these organisations failed to move with the times. Success does not last forever without work and adaptation to a changing socio-economic, political and technological world.

Renewal and growth

One reason for an organisation gradually dying is a failure to renew itself through a healthy story-telling culture. A lot of organisations which fall apart have become demythologised. They have no way of knowing how to move forward because only the old stories and myths of past success continue to be recirculated. When there is no new thinking in the organisation new stories are not generated. In turn, this means people have no basis for recognising opportunities to change things for the better. Typically, inner-directed organisations have unchanging missions and strategic goals that remain unrevised for many years. Although the values of these organisations may stay unchanged, the implementation of those values becomes increasingly difficult when best practices in other organisations are not known or understood.

If 'knowledge (or information) is power', then story-telling is an empowering process. Through story-telling we learn how to 'go with the flow'. No change is terrifying when we are prepared for it. Richard Hames suggested there are three stages of organisational growth, very much like stages of growth in humans.[14] In the first stage—the 'formative phase'—people explore the system in order to find acceptable and repeatable patterns of communicating. This is a time of role differentiation and clarification, as well as a search for meaningful purpose in these roles and the responsibilities which go with them.

During the second, 'normative', stage members of organisations assess all new information against the criteria for repeatable communicating patterns developed in the formative phase. At this stage of an organisation's development, members have the power to make or break the system. One of the traps companies fall into is thinking that their history of success is justification enough to remain static, continuing to do all the good things they have already been doing. While, in one sense, it may be sensible to 'stick to one's knitting'—focusing on what the particular organisation does well—there is the corresponding danger of smugness in assuming that once you've reached the top you'll always stay there. All of us know there is no guarantee of this.

A 'shock to the system' signals the third stage of organisational growth. At this point the acceptance of change is virtually non-negotiable. Changes may have evolved from existing practices or alternatively may involve entirely new approaches to conducting the work of the organisation. Constantly feeding information into the system keeps it alive. Because information sharing is facilitated by a healthy story-telling organisation, the whole system may change or there may be changes to parts within the system. A difficult problem arises, however, when only part of the system feels the 'shock' and the rest of the organisation seems totally immune. Visionaries who have tried to change things despite the apathy of many of the organisation's members have often felt impotent and demoralised. For leaders there is no more frustrating or helpless experience than trying to give vision to those who are blind to workplace realities.

Receptivity to new ideas

Organisational change, therefore, is optimal when the system's culture is open to new ideas which gain currency through the sharing of stories. There are classic instances where organisations failed to grasp and run with new ideas when the opportunities were there. For example, the motor vehicle manufacturing industry in Australia lost a golden opportunity to be a world leader when it decided not to develop or produce a version of the revolutionary Sarich orbital engine. Another scientific discovery dismissed in Australia was a technique for generating rain in clouds. The idea was warmly received in America where the technique is now applied as standard practice during times of drought. Similarly, although the desalination of sea water is a relatively inexpensive process, no one in Australia has taken the initiative to construct a desalination plant. In a country stricken so often by weather extremes, it seems incomprehensible that these opportunities were not seized instantly.

By contrast, story-telling organisations with a culture receptive to open communication with customers have stood out because of their service or product quality. Apple Macintosh computers have made remarkable progress in meeting client needs through the user-friendly interface of their products.

They have stayed very close to their customers, listening to their stories and acting on this communication.

In some story-telling organisations, customers may be directly invited to tell their stories. A good example is JAG Electronics, which services and repairs audio and video hi-fi equipment. After each service or repair job, customers are invited to complete a brief survey on how effective the service has been, and are asked for any suggestions which could make the service even better. Brief questionnaires have also been put to good effect in hotel chains like Holiday Inn and Hilton. In many cases, it has been obvious that staying close to the customer has paid off—one could hardly fault the service given. In higher education and training, the seeking of participant feedback has now become standard practice.

Symbols and leadership

Myths which emerge from the communication or the powerful actions of leaders can have a noticeable impact on the culture of organisations. Hackman and Johnson, for example, cite the story of Fred Meyer, owner of a large food and merchandise retail company in America's northwest.[15] Meyer was renowned for his intolerance of extravagance by his staff. One day, on a visit to one of his stores, he spotted a two metre high stack of coffee jars on a shelf. This was against company policy, because customers would find it hard to reach the product. With a swoop of his cane Meyer knocked all the jars on the shelf to the floor where they smashed. His employees soon learned that, for him, customer service was even more important than curtailing unnecessary expenditure. Through this myth, a new value became part of the culture of Fred Meyer's organisation.

Meyer's symbolic act using his cane reinforces Tom Peters' observation that

> ... [t]he best leaders, especially in chaotic conditions (effective generals, leaders of revolutions), almost without exception and at every level, are master users of stories and symbols.[16]

Many of the world's leading figures, for instance, create a 'sense of the dramatic' when addressing audiences or during some historical moment. When the Pope arrives on foreign soil, his customary first action is to kiss the ground. In launching a new ship, the official speaker flings a bottle of champagne against the hull on conclusion of the speech. Winston Churchill's victory sign, Fidel Castro's fatigues, General Douglas MacArthur's famous corn cob pipe all create a dramatic image which inspired many thousands of people, and make them instantly recognisable. Good managers, too, know how to use dramatic effect to the best advantage of the organisation. Their symbolic actions and communication become the material of new myths recounted by their staff.

Some of the ways in which myths and story-telling can influence the corporate culture of systems have now been considered. While all story-tellers can contribute in some way to an organisation's culture, leaders have the potential to change radically the prevailing values of the system. With culture change of this kind, the communication and actions of staff are likely to be modified as well. In the next section, we'll see how story-telling can help us to understand and manage the 'shadow side' of organisations.

The shadow side and covert culture

Of all subjects managers want to master, dealing with the 'shadow side' remains the most perplexing and disturbing. It is one of the most important competencies managers need to develop. Yet strangely, very little is known about shadow side activities in organisations, largely because researchers have found it much easier, tidier and logically simpler to study more overt aspects of human systems. One person who has given this subject attention, however, is Gerard Egan. He defines the shadow side of a company or institution as the

> *... factors that affect, either positively or negatively, organisational productivity and quality of work life in substantive and systematic ways but are not found in organisational charts or in organisational manuals and are not discussed in the formal or official forums of the institution.*[17]

Since much of the story-telling in organisations occurs informally through daily conversations among members, some of the stories told will impinge on people's productivity or quality of work life. Those stories that do find a mark in the shadow side may often have, among other things, the following characteristics:

- a degree of 'arationality'
- a 'hidden agenda'
- an element of 'office (or organisational) politics'
- a discernible level of emotional involvement
- restricted fantasy themes or types.

Arationality

'Arational' story themes or plots are neither rational nor irrational. People's behaviours or events in stories are often difficult to explain or interpret. When people communicate or act arationally, there is no sure way of predicting what they are about to say or do. Why do individuals quit their jobs for no apparent reason? What causes people to become enemies at work? Are there any explanations for certain power blocks or coalitions forming in the workplace? Why do persons pass notes to each other at committee or board meetings?

Because the arational usually occurs unexpectedly, there is virtually nothing we can do to prevent it. Since the real motives and intentions underlying stories with limited circulation are known only to the story-tellers and sometimes the story-listeners, perceptions of arationality apply only to organisational members outside the story-telling circle. These outsiders typically guess at why certain things appear to be happening and in turn these speculations become the stories of an alternative organisational subculture. Within subcultures, stories and myths can be so powerful as to make stories from other parts of the organisation appear irrelevant, inappropriate and 'undiscussable'.

Gerard Egan believes that a common everyday example of arationality is the failure to live up to contracts. A rational view of contracts would be that they should and will be honoured. Unfortunately, when the contracts are signed promises are easier made than kept. Couples entering matrimony have every intention of making it work but they have little idea of what the relationship will be like years down the track. As Egan observes, 'contracts are human instruments permeated by human strength and human frailty'.[18]

Part III: Building the story-telling organisation

Arational rivalry

An instance of arational communication occurred some years ago in an organisation that was not very people-oriented. Every decision was made on the basis of 'what was best for the system'. Most of the employees thought of the system as an organisational hierarchy represented on a flow chart, rather than as a networked interdependent group of people. And it was not hard to see why they thought like this. They did not act as a team. Individuals complained about each other endlessly. Staff factions demarcated worker from worker. Colleagues squabbled and fought interminably. Some people refused to work on the same projects with certain others. Bitter rivalries which had arisen years ago continued to simmer.

Having noticed this going on for some weeks, one employee suggested to his superior that the staff needed help in developing interpersonal communication skills. His reaction was dumbfounding. He shuffled about a bit, avoided looking at his employee and eventually changed the subject without ever having attempted an answer to the question. A few days later the puzzled employee told a close colleague and friend the story of his meeting with the manager. This story sharing helped him to understand why his suggestion was dismissed without any comment. According to his friend, their superior had a reputation for creating and enjoying conflict with staff. In fact, he didn't want his subordinates to become better communicators; rather, he wanted them to remain ignorant of the advantage of having well-developed people skills. As time went on, the employee began to realise even more why his superior thought like this—he was such a poor communicator himself that even he didn't know what it took to be a good one. To this very day, that manager continues to downplay the importance of communication skills.

When the manager in question first demonstrated his lack of regard for people skills, there seemed to be no obvious reason for it. At this point, his attitude seemed arational. Nevertheless, over time, and with the benefit of frequent story sharing with colleagues to establish an open story-telling culture, the manager's effect on the shadow side culture of the organisation diminished. He had effectively sanctioned as 'normal' the staff's now established behavioural patterns of playing politics, caucusing with like-minded staff against opponent factions and gaining personal advantage by cutting someone else down to size. Eventually, his hidden agenda was exposed.

An understanding of this covert culture gave one employee what he needed to develop a strategy for handling shadow side communication or behaviour directed towards him in the future.

The hidden agenda

Another lesson learned from this experience was that underlying someone's apparent arational conduct is very probably a 'hidden agenda'. In the manager's case, his secret agenda was to ensure that the entire staff of the organisation would not become a co-operative team because their motive for getting together would most likely be to form a solid opposition to him and his regime. A united staff would become their superior's enemy and their unity would spring from a practically unanimous dislike of him and his scheming nature. So long as he kept the staff fighting among themselves, their energies would be directed away from him. His hidden agenda was revealed by observing his communication with his staff over a number of years. Most of his employees eventually arrived at the same conclusion quite independently. As the open story-telling culture of the organisation gradually grew stronger, shared perceptions exposed the myth of an ineptly tyrannical manager.

Empire builders within organisations often have hidden agendas. By not disclosing their stories, ambitious leaders can plan to have things happen to their advantage without others becoming aware of their schemes. Sometimes this may mean subtly undermining a potential competitor's pet projects or goals. A common tactic is to make a rival believe that you are a friend and that you are prepared to support a proposal at the next executive committee meeting. When the time comes, however, you withdraw your support on some pretext like 'things have changed since I spoke with you last'. If we consider this undermining tactic from the deceiver's point of view it is a very rational, calculated and deliberate move. On the other hand, the victim of the deception would find it very difficult to find a reasonable explanation for the deceiver's change of heart.

Organisational politics

Organisational politics also form a significant part of a system's shadow side. Much of the politicking is done 'behind the scenes' through lobbying for support regarding a particular enterprise or project. Other reasons for office politics include vying for power, competing for territory or resources, or changing the culture to fit a particular ideological stance. Generally, members who are not directly involved in political powerplays tend to be aware that something is going on. What they don't know is the precise nature of the political football. Under these circumstances, a 'culture of political uncertainty' can develop within organisations. The remedy for this is the encouragement of open story-telling. Political activities in organisations are practically unavoidable, but open story-telling reduces political uncertainty by affording the various political brokers an opportunity to align their politics with the organisation's strategic mission and goals.

Unfortunately, in many organisations this is more difficult to achieve than one at first may think and will consume many hours of bargaining and conflict between different political subgroups. One result of such bargaining is the reallocation of resources to the political winners. Noel Tichy suggested that organisations vary in their degree of political uncertainty because of changing environments, changing organisational goals and changing opportunities to achieve those goals. One conclusion he drew was that '. . . as political uncertainties increase, so does the need for political bargaining and exchange'.[19] Political bargaining reduces uncertainties in an organisation's culture in proportion to increasing opportunities for open story-telling.

Emotional involvement

Shadow side activity may also be inferred when people in organisations display strong feelings and emotions. It is very natural to feel angry, humiliated, frustrated or vengeful when someone has 'put one over you'. On such occasions, people who have been duped have been starved of stories capable of providing sufficient information to create a defence against emotional outbursts once the deception has been exposed. Such stories could have given clues about potentially harmful situations to be faced in the future.

Not all displays of emotion, however, are due exclusively to shadow side activity. Expressing feelings is very human and natural. Sometimes we can become emotional about things which are openly happening. You may not like the way in which your organisation is being restructured. Your colleagues may resent the addition of new criteria for promotion because they think they are doing much more than a fair workload at the moment. Such circumstances as these can cause us to react publicly with strong feelings. Most likely, however, knowing in advance what's in store for us, we won't get so steamed up when the time comes.

Restricted fantasy types

In shadow side story-telling, knowledge of the fantasy themes and types tends to be confined to the shadow side *operators*. The extreme example of shadow side operators is the 'organisational mafia' that controls the action in some systems. When dominant personalities in organisations are also perceived as opinion leaders within their organisations, they may exercise great power by achieving their goals through a covert subculture.

Fantasy themes and types may relate to the success of this organisational mafia or to the downfall of its enemies. As such, these types remain the private property of the mafia members. Other people in the system may well be aware of the mafia, without correspondingly knowing what its members are up to or plotting.

Dealing with covert action

To understand and manage the shadow side of their organisations, story-tellers need to be able to do the following:

- keep their ears to the ground
- develop a network of reliable story-tellers who corroborate suspected facts
- detect and reject 'crap'.

Keeping one's ear to the ground not only requires infiltrating the story-telling groups in other subcultures of the organisation but also watching for any visible signs of change within the system. These signs can be seen in simple changes to usual or daily routines. For example, when an employee who has regularly taken lunch breaks in the company staff lounge has not been seen there for several days straight. Or again, when certain individuals have become as 'thick as thieves' and are constantly seen chatting over a cup of coffee. Such observed behaviours become the subjects of new stories we may form and share with others.

Part III: Building the story-telling organisation

Sharing our stories with others we know enables us to maintain a network of story-tellers who can verify our suspicions as fact or otherwise. All of us have our own biases and perceptual filters. It's possible that we often see what we want to see rather than what is actually happening. When we check our perceptions with those of our fellow story-tellers, we can get some idea of how accurately we understand our organisation's culture. The more people can confirm our beliefs, the more these beliefs confirm realities. Accurate understanding of one's organisational culture, including its shadow side, is a preliminary step to finding appropriate strategies to manage it.

The third step in understanding the culture of our organisations is the detection and rejection of stories with no basis of fact. Ernest Hemmingway, the famous American author, was once asked what the most essential ability a successful writer should possess. His reply was that any great writer needs 'a built-in, shockproof crap detector'. This piece of wisdom inspired Neil Postman and Charles Weingartner to remark that

> ... one way of looking at the history of the human group is that it has been a continuing struggle against the veneration of 'crap'.[20]

This struggle also goes on in the story-telling organisation. Experienced story-tellers need to find ways of differentiating junk from important information which can lead to changes for the better through inspired story-telling.

Organisations can become overwhelmed with non-essential, or inaccurate, information, just as computers become infected by viruses. Anne Gilpin has argued that organisations, like other living creatures, can be sickened by 'viruses' attacking the body.[21]

Vigilance coupled with counteractive story-telling, therefore, are a good combination for attacking organisational viruses and managing the shadow side. Now we'll consider the next step—how to build an actively positive culture in our organisations through story-telling.

Creating a positive organisational culture

While managing the shadow side of our organisations is a vital and integral part of communicative and story-telling competence, it is not all that we, as model story-tellers, need to know. The ultimate proof of our success as story-tellers is the state of health of our story-telling organisations. A corporate culture which fosters productivity and a good quality of work life is one index of a healthy story-telling system.

There are a number of different things we can do to ensure that our organisations have cultures that benefit their clients and members. One strategy is to provide appropriate training for all members of the system to advise management of desirable and necessary changes. This is something we will focus exclusively on in Chapter 6. For the moment, however, the important question we need to ask ourselves is—'What can we do personally to contribute to building and maintaining a culture reflective of a healthy story-telling organisation?' Four things in particular that we can do are:

- encourage institution-enhancing politics, not the politics of self-interest
- reward rather than punish people for open story-telling
- ensure that stories are shared by all members of the organisation, regardless of their place on the corporate ladder
- capitalise on existing myths and stories to guide the strategic thinking of leaders and lead to worthwhile changes by communicating values.

The politics of institutional enhancement

Whether we like it or not, organisational politics will always have an influence on the culture of our systems. No organisation is totally free of internal politics. Colleagues may often be heard saying 'I don't want to know' when confronted with the pressure to take sides in a conflict. But fence-sitters of this kind are mostly in a minority and in any case contribute little towards a healthy corporate culture because they refuse to be part of the story-telling network.

Gerard Egan suggests that if we have to play politics we should at least try to use politics that are institution-enhancing rather than institution-limiting.[22] The important question is not 'What's in it for me?', but rather 'How is this going to help all of us as a team?'

Promoting the politics of institutional enhancement may be difficult if the existing culture in our organisation has been built and rooted in the politics of self-interest.

Rewards for speaking out

We also need to reward people for speaking out and stating their points of view. As small scale replicas of the larger society in which they are embedded, organisations tend to espouse the values of the wider system. In countries where freedom of speech is part of the constitution or political culture, organisations which value this principle are more likely to have an open story-telling culture than one which operates typically through the shadow side. Unfortunately, organisations are not always supportive of free speech. Part of this has been due to those agitating for 'politically correct' speech, which opposes discrimination against people of different ethnic backgrounds, religions or gender. Within organisations, the 'antipols' who do not sympathise with the demand for politically correct speech have often 'gone underground', using the shadow side to express their prejudices.

While we would not want to give the antipols complete licence to derogate others in their organisations, encouraging them to share their stories in an atmosphere that is non-threatening or non-punitive is a tactic more likely to engender attitude change than some institutional policy prohibiting specific ways of thinking or speaking. One obvious non-threatening place is the training room, where stories can be shared as part of a learning experience and not subjected to disciplinary action by participants' superiors. We have more to say about this in the next chapter. Another approach might be for managers to speak informally with offending persons, advising them to avoid speech which insults or upsets others in the system. In this way, politically incorrect communicators would have a chance to modify their choice of words in future on the tacit understanding that previous offences would be forgotten. Naturally, persisting offenders would need to be warned or officially disciplined.

Speaking across organisational boundaries

A third step we can take is to ensure that at every level of the organisation's hierarchy members know what is going on. There is nothing more aggravating than discovering decisions after they have been implemented.

> Years ago a number of school teachers became very angry that they had not been consulted regarding a statewide teachers' strike. The industrial union executives had taken the view that as the elected representatives of all teachers

> in the state, they could decide what actions the entire union membership should take. No meetings of teachers were held. Instead, there was an announcement on a national radio station that all teachers would be on strike for 24 hours on the Tuesday of the following week. On the day of the strike, less than 10 per cent of the members of the teachers' union turned up at stop work meetings in different locations throughout the state. The majority went to their schools where it was business as usual.

In large corporate organisations it is a mistake to think that stories invariably make their way to the top or to the bottom of the ladder. Many CEOs and their senior entourages simply don't know how people down the line think or feel. Similarly, in organisations whose structure is not 'flat', rank-and-file members may have little idea of what their bureaucratic managers are planning. The key to a healthy story-telling organisation is in providing all members access to any story in the system. Managers who 'manage by walking around' (MBWA) are more likely to hear the stories told by their subordinates than those who 'rule from on high'. People who have MBWA managers can contribute to a positive story-telling climate by sharing stories which their managers could act on for everyone's benefit.

Building on existing mythology

Some stories may be more important to the organisation than others because they can help in the leadership of change. Myths about archetypal heroes in the organisation are one example. The success stories of former leaders can teach current managers a lot about approaches and tactics that are likely to work or not work.

> When nursing education ceased to be hospital-based and was moved into universities in some states of Australia, there was predictably a negative reaction on the part of some senior hospital-based nurse educators. They argued that a university-based nurse education program would be too theoretical. The only way nurses could learn to do their work properly was on the job. If this meant spending the first three months of their training doing nothing else but washing out bedpans until they could do this in their sleep, then this is what they should do.

Part III: Building the story-telling organisation

> Many stories from both hospital-based and university-based nurse educators and students were openly exchanged over the next few years. In some cases, either side was proved to be true. For example, one university decided that trainee nurses should have a liberal education. So nurses there actually undertook a major subject sequence in English literature. By the end of the degree course, the graduate nurses could quote a good deal from Shakespeare but had real trouble connecting a drip to a patient. Alternatively, the university trained nurses in many instances appeared clearly more articulate than their previously hospital trained counterparts. Some claimed patients seemed to find it easier communicating with the 'new breed' of nurses than with the 'old breed'.

The point of this story is that through the exchange of stories about both the present and former systems of nurse education, valuable lessons were learned and the best features of hospital-based and university-based training were identified. Hospital-based nurse education produced nurses who had superior technical and practical skills, whereas university-based nurse education turned out nurses who could, in the absence of direct advice from medical practitioners, more confidently make clinical judgments about patient care. Subsequently, university nurse education curricula were revised to include the best features of both systems. The result was highly gratifying to nurse education authorities. Today, nurse education in Australia is at the international forefront.

To help sustain a healthy story-telling culture, we should learn from the organisation's existing mythology and use its lessons to perpetuate myth-making as inspirational opportunities arise. Above all, we must not lose the art of creating myths. This is very easy to do in a world that is becoming more and more materialistic and pragmatic. Organisations without myths lose a vital 'life quality' and become mechanical. When an organisation's vision is limited to the practicalities of the present, there is little room for strategic leadership.

Summary

Myth-making and story-telling create 'cultural wells' from which change agents can draw new ideas. These wells dry up once people cease to care for or nurture the mythologies of their organisations. Just as leaders need a source of stimulation for their creative thinking, those who follow need confidence in their leaders' choice of direction. Shared myths in organisations that have a healthy story-telling culture can thus go a long way to reducing the uncertainties of the members.

In this chapter we journeyed into the world of organisational culture. After we explored the nature and dimensions of organisational culture, we learned how myths and story-telling contribute to corporate culture. We reminded ourselves that within organisations there is a 'shadow side' as well as an open culture. We saw that it is important to understand the shadow side of our own organisations, since such understanding can assist us in managing change even through shadow side activities. Most significantly, we ventured beyond the street fighting tactics common among many shadow side operators, to learning how to build a positive, open, healthy story-telling culture in our organisations. In Chapter 6, we'll discover ways of helping people to build such cultures as a result of developing some of the critical skills of story-telling and story-listening.

6

developing the art of story-telling

We live mythically but continue to think fragmentarily and on single planes.
Marshall McLuhan

Now that we have ventured into the world of story-telling and myth, we are probably asking ourselves 'What can we do to help ourselves and others become more skilled as story-tellers and story-listeners?'. What are the skills we need to develop? And how can we be sure that what we learn through training will help us in our organisational life? Our focus in Chapter 6, therefore, is on workplace training and on creating a staff development approach that will help us (and our consultants) become comfortable and adept in story-telling and myth interpretation.

Managers as story-tellers and story-listeners

Understanding myths and story-telling in organisations is a first and very necessary step for us to become competent story-tellers and story-listeners. We do not become experts in story-telling, however, just by understanding the nature of a story-telling organisation. What we, as managers, need to do is identify our story-telling roles in our organisation. Then we can work out the abilities we'll require in order to carry out those roles successfully. These abilities could range from skills in public speaking to critical thinking about mythical themes and the lessons we can learn from them.

The manager's roles

As a manager you may fulfil the role of an 'administrator' at times, approving staff leave applications or departmental expenditure, among other things. Alternatively, you may act as a 'helper', assisting your colleagues to accomplish their tasks successfully, to achieve their goals or to contribute to the implementation of the department's strategic plan. Sometimes you may need to wear the hat of an 'adviser' or 'counsellor', listening with empathy to individuals telling you about their troubles and emotional problems. To some of your staff you may be a 'mentor'—they will use you as a role-model to pattern their own communication and actions. As managers, therefore, we perform a variety of roles.

It is difficult not to think of any of these managerial roles as story-telling or story-listening ones. In a sense, everything a manager does or says tells a story. Seven roles, however, are singled out because of their importance for most story-telling situations in which managers are likely to find themselves:

- the team leader/builder/giver of direction
- the harmoniser/conflict resolver
- the 'open information source' or censor
- the motivator/inspirer/energiser/persuader
- the staff developer
- the public relations/spokesperson
- the 'defender of the faith'.

Team leader
As team leaders and builders, managers are both story-tellers and story-listeners. Among other things, team leaders need to communicate their vision to the group through persuasive story-telling. The team members will be co producing the scripts as they clarify and probe the leader's basic story-line.

Part III: Building the story-telling organisation

In large organisations, there could be many teams making up the system. All these follow a common mission and show their commitment to it by performing their particular roles to the best of their ability. In so doing, they are telling their own stories, which give credibility to the 'grand myth', or mission statement. The Sydney Adventist Hospital serves as a good example. Its mission statement reads like this:

> The Sydney Adventist Hospital is a Christian institution operated by the Seventh-day Adventist Church. We believe in the uniqueness of the individual, created in the likeness of God. We are committed to the Christian ethic of respect for each person's worth and dignity.
>
> OUR MISSION IS
> - to provide care focused on the nurture and healing of the whole person;
> - to maintain a standard of excellence in all services;
> - to make optimal use of resources and technology;
> - to educate in the principles of healthful living and disease prevention;
> - to encourage and assist all staff to attain the highest personal and professional standards.[1]

All patients at this hospital are given a copy of a publicity brochure with this mission statement. The pages that follow the mission statement tell a number of stories about how the various teams can make it happen. The Sydney Adventist Hospital's public relations document is a stunning example of how to tell the story of a genuinely interdependent team effort.

While leaders publicise externally the achievements of their teams in brochures, much of their story-telling occurs in team meetings or with individual members of the team. To tell outsiders the true story of their team, leaders need to spend time with their staff, listening carefully to the stories of all team members, so that they can retell these accurately to clients or customers. Armed with this knowledge, leaders can work out how best to communicate their vision to the team and how to secure the team's commitment to the realisation of that vision. The question leaders should ask themselves is 'What's the best way I can tell my story of how this team can become a legend in its time?'.

Conflict resolver

When teams do not behave like teams but rather as a collection of skirmishing individuals, managers are greatly advantaged if they can perform the role of conflict resolver or harmoniser. To do this well, managers will need to call upon their story-telling and story-listening skills once more.

Managers must remember to:

- listen impartially to stories from both sides in dispute
- script a 'harmonious team story' that is more appealing than the present scenario of dissension among members.

'Cowboy' managers tend to shoot from the hip. They are prepared to fire shots before they know the full facts of the story. Often cowboy managers are tempted to act on a complaint immediately—without finding out the whole story. By acting at once, even if it is precipitous to do so, some managers feel they give the impression of being 'doers' and not fence-sitters. When their disciplinary actions prove to be inappropriate and unnecessary, however, their credibility is 'shot to pieces'. A wise manager always listens non-judgmentally to both conflicting parties before scripting a solution that creates as little difficulty to either side as possible.

One way to do this is to visualise a harmonious team and then craft a story on this visualisation. This story is then told to the team as an intended learning experience. There is no certainty, of course, that this will work. When people get locked into a mind set about a dispute, often very little will change their attitude to their opponents.

Imagine taking charge of an organisation where bitter in-fighting between certain members has been going on for years. The stories of some of these conflicts become part of the organisation's mythology. In situations like these, where interpersonal resentments have been running high for a long time, treating the conflicting staff members to a harmonious team story may be like offering membership of a society of conscientious objectors to top ranking officers in the armed services. All that team leaders can do when there is such an impasse is to sell the 'let's agree to disagree' story to those in conflict. With much to get done in the organisation, managers should try to help staff keep personal conflicts out of team-based activities. However, effective conflict resolvers need to be aware that there is a shadow side to organisational life and culture, just as we noted earlier on. While it is desirable to keep personal conflicts to a minimum, the reality of office politics needs to be acknowledged. In other words, harmonising works well when it is reality-tested. There is little point in trying to get people to work harmoniously together if political realities have not been addressed. In some instances, conflict may be averted more reliably by judiciously keeping certain people apart.

Information gatekeeper

Managers also have to decide how much of the voluminous information they receive should be passed along to their staff. Many managers make a point of passing to their subordinates every piece of information they get. One effect this has is to ensure that much of the descending information is relegated to the garbage bin. Some employees resent receiving information of this kind, believing that their managers are reneging on making tough decisions and on standing by these even if the consequences are not pleasant.

On the other hand, some managers believe in protecting their staff from the paper war by giving them information only on the so-called 'need to know' basis. The danger here is that managers can easily slip into the role of 'censor'. If in doubt about which way to go, managers are probably best advised to opt for keeping their staff completely informed at all times of what's happening in the organisation. That way there is less pretext for staff to work the shadow side or engage in arational story-telling. When staff are kept abreast of developments in their organisation, they have the opportunity to react and tell their own stories, regardless of whether they choose to do so or not.

Inspirational leader

Many people believe it is the manager's role to motivate staff. There are claims today that the managers who are most successful in motivating their teams are 'inspirational leaders'[2] or 'charismatic leaders'.[3] While charisma is a trait associated with many mythical heroes, it is, according to Leanne Atwater,

Developing the art of story-telling

Robert Penn and Linda Rucker 'not a "god-like" quality, but is one which can be identified and nurtured in leaders in organisations'.[4] Their study showed that charismatic leaders were significantly more dynamic, inspiring, outgoing, sociable, insightful and enterprising than non-charismatic leaders. It was also found that charisma can be learned by observing one's superiors acting as role-models. The researchers noted that:

> [M]anagers tend to copy behaviour they observe in their immediate supervisors. An ideal strategy might be to select top managers who were charismatic, who would in turn influence the managers below them . . .[5]

Inspirational leaders know how to use persuasive appeals in their story-telling to motivate staff. Bass argues that:

> [T]he inspirational leader has to have insight into what will be challenging to a follower and for what reasons . . . There are many different possible behaviours which could be inspirational. The leader could set challenging objectives as standards, use symbols and images cleverly to get ideas across, provide meaning for proposed action, point out reasons why followers will succeed, remain calm in crises, appeal to feelings, call for meaningful actions, stress beating the competition, envision an attractive, attainable future and articulate how to get there.[6]

The key to inspirational leaders' motivation of followers is their ability to use metaphors and symbols when creating their stories, especially when they structure their vision and accompanying 'paradigms of action'. Even if there are internal and external uncertainties and threats to the realisation of their vision, inspirational leaders tend to stick to their optimistic scripts, always on the lookout for opportunities to 'turn unpredictable events into building blocks of change'.[7] For inspirational leaders, story-telling involves the ability to manage meaning. Leaders can interpret complex and ambiguous stories by recasting them in a form which followers will be able to use as a guide for their own story-telling and actions. Even back in the 1970s, Karl Weick was evangelistic in arguing that a manager is primarily a manager of myths, symbols and images.[8]

In large organisations the 'strategic apex' consists of the CEO and an inner circle of high ranking executives at the strategy formulation level. To make decisions for action in a future clouded with uncertainties, strategic apex leaders use 'scripts' which are like intuitive mental pictures made up of stories, myths and organisational folklore. According to Hunt, Baliga and Peterson, scripts serve as

> ... *vivid, emotion-filled, often overly-certain, intuitive guides to strategic decision making in an all-too-uncertain future. Scripts, generated both from personal experiences and the accumulated wisdom of one's culture are largely invisible, only moderately rational and tremendously powerful.*[9]

Inspirational leaders use symbols not only to explain complex or ambiguous meanings in organisational life and culture but also to highlight their authority, status and position. Monarchs, for example, wear crowns and other regalia. Judges in courts of law dress in distinctive gowns and wigs. Senior clergy in the Roman Catholic and Greek or Russian Orthodox Churches can be readily identified by their clothing. In corporate organisations, the symbols of inspirational leaders may be related to 'power dressing' where expensive attire may signal efficiency, authority, power and an image of success.

Two actions associated with motivation and inspiration are 'energising' and 'persuading'. Because inspirational leaders are perceived as dynamic and highly enthusiastic about their work, their whole persona gives the team a 'buzz'. In other words, followers are 'given a charge of energy' through the example of inspiring leaders. Like harmonising, energising is a team building or 'group maintenance' role. Charismatic or inspirational leaders can energise their team by story-telling that stirs their followers' imaginations. Often this story-telling is future-directed. Think of Martin Luther King's famous speech where he said repeatedly 'I have a dream'. His dream was a 'fantasy theme' for a world of peaceful co-existence among people of all races.

As with energising, persuasion is most successful when the manager or leader is a person of high credibility—such a leader is perceived by his or her staff to be expert, trustworthy and dynamic. Through persuasion, workers can be motivated to improve their work for the good of their company. Many people hold the popular misconception that 'persuasion' is a process of manipulating or deceiving others. In fact, persuasion is a very useful ability for managers to develop, since it gives them a means for helping others understand their organisation's culture and strategic directions.

Staff developer
The motivator role of managers relates closely to the staff developer role. Some managers do not see the development of their staff as their responsibility. Generally, these managers are focused tightly on visible task accomplishment and productivity—if sales or production are up, things are going well. Task-oriented managers of this kind rarely understand the influence that highly trained and developed staff can have on productivity and quality performance. Effective team leaders, on the other hand, know how to get the best out of their staff, often by providing them with opportunities to learn through training or other developmental activities, such as gaining work experience for a short intensive period in another part of the organisation.

A lot of staff development occurs as a result of formal story-telling in training rooms, brainstorming sessions with colleagues from one's own department, team meetings facilitated by external consultants or at professional conferences, seminars and workshops under the auspices of well-known bodies.

To perform the staff development role well, managers need to differentiate the activities that will genuinely benefit their staff from those that will make little difference. The best way for managers to become discerning staff developers of this kind is to continue to be active learners themselves, always keeping abreast of the latest developments and thinking in the fields of management and organisational behaviour.

Spokesperson
In a sense managers need to have one foot in their departments and the other in the world outside their part of the system. You can't know the whole story

about your organisation and its external environment by locking yourself into your own sphere of activity. So, another role for managers is in public relations. While managers need to be expert story-tellers in their own departments, they also have an obligation to keep close to the customer or client. This will involve learning the stories of the customers or clients as well as telling them the story of their part in the life and culture of the organisation.

Some of the publicity which managers give out in their public relations role is formal and factual. Annual reports, for example, contain detailed stories of sales, goods produced or services provided by organisations. Publicity, however, may also occur through direct liaison with clients or customers, often on an informal, 'off-the-record' basis. Either way, managers act as spokespersons for their teams, ensuring that the work and expertise of the team is publicised to the advantage of both customers and team members through appropriate and inspired story-telling.

Defender of the faith
Finally, managers need to perform 'the defender of the faith' role. No matter what happens with any task or project, the accountability for the ultimate success or failure of the outcome rests squarely with the manager. When the former US President Harry S. Truman coined the expression 'the buck stops here', he set a precedent for all people in authority. Despite contemporary trends to empower all members of teams, the designated leader is still expected to be the one to bear the consequences of unsatisfactory work carried out by the team. Thus, managers as 'defenders of the faith' should develop the ability to present to their staff a clear picture of performance outcomes that are acceptable. Painting clear word-pictures is another facet of story-telling competence.

So where do we go from here? We have seen that there are at least seven key story-telling roles that managers perform in the course of their work. Now the question is: 'How can managers be helped to perform these roles and the responsibilities that go with them?'. In other words, we must look for an approach to assist managers to learn the art and skills of story-telling.

An approach for training managers

To begin with a caveat, there is no single 'correct' approach for training managers to be good story-tellers. Chip Bell and Fred Margolis have stated that:

> ... [t]raining has many meanings. Its special interpretations are best appreciated through examining its goals.[10]

There may be several equally effective ways of training managers in the art of story-telling. The important thing is to specify as accurately as possible the goals or targets managers need to achieve in order to be seen as competent story-tellers—'as accurately as possible' because story-telling is an art and as such the attainment of any goals in story-telling training may need to be determined somewhat subjectively. Grades or numerical scores for competence in story-telling would not mean very much either to the manager-as-trainee story-teller or to the training facilitator. Perhaps a more appropriate way to examine training goals and whether they are being met is to identify a set of best educational practice guidelines to keep in mind when designing management development programs.

We may do well to test any training approach we may be thinking of using against the following practical criteria:

Criteria for a management development program

- Are the training goals or aims realistic and attainable? Is there enough time to achieve what we are aiming for or should we be planning for a second or more follow-up sessions?

- Are these goals appropriate for the audience in question? Are the participants familiar with the story-telling concept? Are they experienced, mature and competent communicators?

- Is the approach psychologically threatening to the trainees? Do the course members find it difficult to participate in experiential learning techniques like role-playing and sociodrama? Do they get tongue-tied, embarrassed or petrified at exposing their inability to think or communicate spontaneously?

- Could the goals be realised through means other than training? For example, could managers learn about the art of story-telling through a program of self-guided study? Could they then acquire some basic skills through unsupervised practice in story-telling techniques?
- How can the trainees' involvement and commitment to training be optimised? Do the trainees perceive it as potentially useful and beneficial? Is the training a 'fun' experience? Will managers resist training on-the-job because of the temptation to carry on with their normal duties?
- How will we know if the trainees have achieved what they were supposed to have achieved? Has a follow-up of how training participants have changed their on-the-job practices been designed using a challenging, sensitive and innovative investigative methodology?
- How can we be sure that trainees will successfully do on-the-job what they have learned to do in the training room? Should the training be conducted on-the-job rather than in training rooms? Will the training room be seen as an artificial setting for important learning?
- Are the managers-as-trainee story-tellers likely to question the credibility of the trainers or facilitators? Do the trainees feel they can learn more from their superiors than from their training facilitators or from each other?
- What basis for future self-development has the present training given to the trainees? What options have been suggested to the participants for continuing their development in the art and skills of story-telling after training?
- How can we be certain that the learning benefits from the present training approach are long-term and not simply skills that will soon be forgotten?

Keys to effective training

One problem that many managers face is that learning on-the-job is often a stressful or bitter experience and management education and training has given managers little help in learning from distress. As Robin Snell has noted:

> ... management education has offered little to prepare managers to learn from distress. Nor has management education done much to equip managers to adopt, in addition, learning practices that are comparatively free of distress ... many of the managers I interviewed appeared to have remained bewildered 'pupils' in the 'School of Hard

Knocks' and to have become generally disillusioned and demotivated because so much of their learning had stemmed from bitter experience.[11]

A major key to effective training for story-telling is to make the experience as stress-free and non-threatening as possible. Many of us have seen what damage insensitive facilitators can cause by compelling trainees to participate in role-plays and simulation exercises without first preparing participants for what is often a very unfamiliar and uncomfortable kind of experience. Experiential learning can be very powerful but people need to be oriented to it gently and gradually by skilful trainers.

At the 1994 International Organisational Behavior Teaching Conference in Dunedin, New Zealand, two very talented story-tellers demonstrated some story-telling techniques for 'people who work with people in organisations'. Marie Finlay, a professional story-teller and organisational development consultant, and Christine Hogan, a university lecturer with a passionate interest in innovative teaching-learning approaches, described four story-telling exercises:

○ warm-up
○ retelling
○ surfacing the culture of the organisation
○ creating the myth.[12]

These exercises are very basic and designed for people who know little about story-telling in organisations.

The warm-up

The 'warm up' is much like an icebreaker exercise. It is meant to be non-threatening and intended as an enjoyable introduction to story-telling and story-listening. In a typical training session, the session leader or facilitator asks participants to work in pairs. One of the partners is the story-teller and the other the story-listener who takes the role of 'giver of words'. To start with, the giver of words asks the story-teller, 'Tell me a story about . . . ' For example, the story-teller could be asked to tell a story about 'what kind of work you do' or 'the people you admire most in this world'. As the story is being created and told, the story-listener issues cue words or phrases aimed at refocusing the story-line. If, for instance, the story-teller is constructing a story about colleagues at work, the giver of words may simply interrupt with words or phrases like 'best friend' or 'most helpful manager' or 'enemy to be watched'.

This goes for about three minutes, after which members of pairs reverse their roles. When the second story has been told, the training facilitator encourages participants to reflect and discuss points like 'What did you find the most difficult thing to do in this exercise?', and 'Why?'. Ultimately, the members of pairs become part of the whole group and share their insights with everyone else participating in the session. As we can see, right from the very beginning, story-telling training is intended to be a valuable learning experience.

Retelling the story and creating the myth
The other three exercises suggested by Marie Finlay and Christine Hogan are designed to develop particular skills. For example, retelling stories is useful for practising and refining active listening, particularly when the exercise is conducted in groups of three persons. After one person tells the story, the other two link arms and jointly retell the story, emphasising not only the content of the story but also the feelings expressed by the story-teller. As with the first exercise, members of the group take turns at being story-tellers and story-retellers. Evidently, emotions can run high in this exercise when story-tellers hear their stories being retold. To calm any heightened feelings, the facilitator may find it helpful to 'de-brief' the story-tellers by asking questions like 'How did you feel as you were hearing your story retold?' or 'What were you feeling as you were listening to a story you knew you were expected to retell afterwards?'

'Surfacing the culture of the organisation' and 'Creating the myth' are exercises which require story-telling trainees to create images or mind-pictures. This is often done by asking participants to close their eyes, relax and let ideas and images flow freely into the mind. A guiding question might be 'What image comes to your mind when you think of your organisation?'. The image could be something as abstract as a collage of colours or as definite as an object or creature. Sometimes it helps to encourage participants to sketch their image on paper before explaining it to others in the group. A general discussion usually reveals similarities and differences in images conjured up by members of the training group. These exercises suggest that 'surfacing the culture' involves bringing to conscious awareness the cultural elements that guide our thinking and actions in our organisations. Such cultural elements would include, among other things, individual and shared values, standards of acceptable communciation and behaviour, taboos and rules—both written and unwritten. Only when we are fully aware of the cultural forces that drive us are we in a position to decide to be guided by current stories and myths or, alternatively, to create new ones.

Learning by doing

Experienced educators like Marie Finlay and Christine Hogan usually have an extensive repertoire of approaches and techniques to facilitate the learning of training course participants. These can range from instructor-centred approaches like formal lectures or mediated presentations like training videos or films to learner-centred approaches including group discussions and real practice in the skills to be developed. In story-telling training, it is critical that trainees do not only learn what story-telling is all about and how it works but also receive plenty of opportunity to practise telling and listening to stories. While there's no denying that people can acquire some story-telling skills by observing and imitating experienced or inspiring story-tellers, without the chance to practise and do some story-telling, the training will be little more than a consciousness-raising exercise.

Any effective training approach to help people become skilled in story-telling will be based on the assumption that 'learning by doing' is far more powerful than learning by passively receiving information from an authority figure or expert. This does not deny the value of listening to 'gurus'. However, without the reality of having experienced something, people find it naturally difficult to apply words of wisdom to their own lives and interpersonal worlds. Will Rifkin says there are 25 ways to spot an 'expert'. For example, experts differentiate their status from those with whom they are communicating by using visible symbols like medals, badges or ceremonial robes. In this way, they ritualise their relationship with non experts to the point that being shown deference by their audiences appears 'natural' to experts.[13]

The lifelong learning process

One important thing to remember is that developing competence as a story-teller is a lifelong learning process. As managers, we need to disabuse ourselves of the belief, to which we so often fall prey, that competence is achieved by slavishly following a minimal number of simple practical steps. Life is not always simple. Neat, formula-based decisions are not necessarily the best.

Learning to be a story-teller need not be a finite experience, which we check off on our list of managerial competencies when we finish a training course. One way of understanding the lifelong learning nature of story-telling competence is to think of some martial art, like judo or karate. The level of competence one reaches is signified by the colour of the belt worn. Traditionally, the black belt indicates the highest level of learning and achievement in the martial art. Even at this level, people can progress to higher levels of competence, evidenced by 'dans'. A black belt of the seventh dan is thus more highly developed than a black belt of a sixth or lower dan. Note the emphasis on 'art' rather than 'skill'—a martial art is more than a mechanical exercise. At the higher levels of development, there is increasing demand upon one's mental, emotional and spiritual capacities.

Story-telling as an art

Like the martial arts, story-telling is an art—not all art can be taught or learned in formal training rooms. As with exceptional performers in any artistic field, good story-tellers add a personal dimension to their story-telling. Often this personal element is associated with emotions expressed by the story-teller while narrating the story. Story-tellers' expressed feelings give stories an individualistic quality and differentiate them from 'just any other story-teller's story'. Those of us who can recall inspiring or exciting story-tellers may associate some of their accompanying non-verbal characteristics with the powerful impressions we had of the stories we listened to. For example, skilled narrators know how to use their voice to best effect by varying, among other things, the volume, speed, rhythm and inflection of their speech. It's hard to give rules for how to do this well. Much of this is a matter of sensitivity, particularly sensitivity to audience reactions to the unfolding tale.

Any successful approach in helping managers to become good story-tellers will also recognise that story-telling is a creative part of the process of communication. This means that both the story-teller and the story-listener are involved in building shared or reciprocated meanings about the story-line, the story's setting and characters, and the moral or lesson to be learned from the story. It is in the story-teller's interest to check that the story-listener received the story as intended, especially if the story is part of the formal professional activity of the organisation. To get a story wrong may be tantamount to unwittingly sabotaging the system's mission and goals.

Practice in the communication of stories is a necessary and critical component of the story-teller's training and development. All kinds of stories should be practised so that in real workplace situations each story is presented in as perfected and polished a form as possible. It is better to fumble and stumble over the telling of a story in the training room rather than back at work. Regardless of whether the story is spoken or written, corrective or confirmatory feedback will help the trainee manager-as-story-teller to present the story well on-the-job. This feedback on practice story-telling and story-listening can come from fellow participant trainees or from expert resources like the training facilitator. If given constructively, such feedback should not be threatening but perceived as part of useful learning applicable to the manager's real professional and interpersonal world.

Managing resistance

Inevitably, some managers resent and resist opportunities for management training and development. Sometimes there is good reason for such resistance. Previously attended management development programs may have been poorly designed and conducted. As a result, managers may have felt their time was being wasted and that it could have been put to better use back on-the-job. Henry Culley saw this as one of three factors that block and create resistance to participation in management development:

- managers tend to be preoccupied with what they leave behind when they attend training and with what will be waiting for them when they return to the job
- managers tend to be action-oriented and very sensitive to demands on their time

○ managers may simply have a bias against training and development, especially in organisations where training is fairly 'mechanical' and limited to the acquisition of basic supervisory skills.[14]

With these in mind, Culley enunciated a general principle of program design: *a development program has to provide a level of stimulation and learning equal to or greater than the experience available in participants' workplace or from their work.*[15] To do this, program designers and trainers must remember the following point: managers are highly motivated to perform when they feel they are being 'treated as professionals' and 'have autonomy in decision-making'.[16] One way training facilitators can treat managers as professionals is to apply relevant adult learning principles and goals in the design of story-telling skills programs.

Outcomes

In today's world of practicalities, people will want to know the outcomes of training in story-telling. Outcomes, however, are not always easily measured. For example, it is highly probable that trained story-tellers will have intensified their passion and enthusiasm for story-telling as an instructional tool for learning about organisational communication, behaviour and culture. How do we quantify any increase in such passion? Similarly, is audience appreciation an outcome? Should loudness of the applause be the measure? The outcomes of story-telling training are best appraised subjectively by the facilitator, the trained story-teller and by future story-listeners.

Adult learning goals

Adult learning goals must be distinguished from adult learning principles for two reasons: firstly, there are very few empirically supported adult learning 'principles' and, secondly, what some adult educators would call 'principles' are more correctly or appropriately labelled adult learning 'goals' or 'desired outcomes'. For example, becoming a self-directed learner is, for adults, a goal. There is no certainty or principle that all adults become self-directed learners. Many adults depend on formal communication with others to broaden their thinking and extend their learning. Increasingly, today's universities have enormous demands from experienced, mature-aged managers for places in MBAs and other human resource-oriented courses. Of course, this does not deny that some dedicated and professionally disciplined managers do learn and develop just as effectively in less formal self-directed ways.

By contrast, 'lifelong learning' is a principle rather than a goal. While some people make the most of every opportunity to learn from their experiences in life, others may apppear to change very little as a result of daily circumstances or events. No matter how small the change is, it signals that learning has taken place. It is a fact of life that through story-telling and listening in their organisations, people learn, change their ways of thinking and behaviour and, as a result, develop their competence as communicators. Story-telling educators and trainers should bear this in mind. In one sense, training for story-telling should be easy and straightforward because it is about what really happens wherever people work together. Most managers will find it exciting to increase their understanding of what they do and what really takes place in their working lives by developing and practising the skills of story-telling and story-listening.

Communicating training assumptions

A story-telling skills training approach based on adult learning goals and principles usually rests on a number of assumptions about the participants, the facilitator and the training course. Some typical assumptions about the participants include:

- The participants will learn most effectively when they are goal-directed (that is, they have developed reasons for what they are doing).
- The participants will take responsibility for the success or failure of their own learning.
- The learning gains of the participants will be proportional to the amount of effort they put into the training course; participants need to be active learners; the learning experience will not be as powerful if participants expect to be 'spoon-fed' by the trainer.
- The participants will think critically about their professional experiences, linking theoretical insights to actual practice.

- Each participant brings a special kind of experience and expertise to the group of trainees; the sharing of this experience and expertise with other participants creates a valuable resource to peers in the group.
- The participants should realise that developing competence in story-telling goes beyond this training course; learning is a lifelong process; this training course is only another starting point in that process.

To complement these, we can assume two things about the facilitator (or trainer):

- The facilitator is essentially a helper. Facilitators, therefore, cannot 'transfer' or 'impart' their story-telling skills to trainees. In other words, facilitators cannot learn something for someone else.
- The facilitator serves as a special resource for the participants. As a specialist in understanding story-telling and human communication, the facilitator can raise the participants' awareness of what to strive for and how to do it.

Finally, it is important that participants understand the assumptions underlying the story-telling training course or program:

- The story-telling training course should not be seen as a 'bible' but rather as a stimulus and guide for further thinking, reading and self-directed inquiry.
- The course is neither good nor bad in itself. It is as good or bad as the participants want to make it.
- The course maximises opportunities for participants to share their expertise and experience and to learn from each other. In this way, participants will benefit from the chance to swap stories that are professionally relevant and real.
- The course encourages participants to work as a group and to address specific training tasks as group problem-solving activities.
- The course is designed to enable participants to become aware of the nature and skills of story-telling. The development and refinement of story-telling competence is very much in the hands of the course participants.

Communicating these assumptions to managers at the very start of a training program or course seems to make the training go more smoothly. Most participants see these assumptions as the trainer's expectations of them and, with very rare exceptions, they live up to them. This is a clear example of the 'Pygmalion Effect'—participants will behave or perform according to the trainer's manifest image, impression or expectation of them. If a group of adult learners believes that they are seen as mature, responsible and hard-working, this is how they'll perform in the course. In short, expectations become a self-fulfilling prophecy.

Measuring success

How will we know if the story-telling training has been successful? Can we notice any changes in the managers participating in the story-telling training program and are these changes making any difference to their performance in the workplace over time? 'Over time' is stressed, because some managers may initially appear to be totally unmoved or untouched by exposure to the world of story-telling.

The initial reaction may even be dismissive. At the conclusion of one session, Ken, a participant who was a human resource development consultant to a government department denounced the story-telling concept as a load of airy-fairy rubbish. This person was an archetypal no-nonsense manager who only had time for practical, 'real' and useful matters. However, months later, he contacted the author to find out when *Myth-makers and Story-tellers* will be published. Ken is excited by the way story-telling helped him understand how to be a more sensitive and purposeful manager. Today he is anxious to become even better at managing his staff through good story-telling. There is a growing network of people interested in story-telling and he is keen to be part of it. Ken's changed attitude to story-telling, moreover, is by no means unique. It will take time for many other task-oriented managers to realise there is a human side to management and that developing people skills through story-telling makes task accomplishment easier and more pleasurable.

With changes in managers' attitude also comes changes in their behaviour. Generally, people can perceive behavioural changes in managers when communication and relationships with those they supervise noticeably improve. In turn, communication between managers and their staff can be seen to be working well when there is a healthy open story-telling culture and staff rarely use or resort to the shadow side. The climate in the workplace is perceived by employees to be not only 'psychologically safe' and non-threatening but also genuinely supportive of staff initiative and innovation. The emergence of an organisation's non-threatening climate often corresponds with mutual respect and understanding among the members of the system. And this happens when the art of story-telling is uppermost in the minds of people working together.

Extending managers' learning

Non-training approaches to helping managers develop the art and skills of story-telling have not been considered. While there is, in today's world of management, a growing interest in story-telling, many other managers think it a waste of time to read a book like this one. These no-nonsense managers cannot accept the practicality, reality and inevitability of story-telling in organisations. Without being required to undergo training in story-telling, they are most unlikely to choose to broaden their thinking and understanding of organisational life by reading any literature on story-telling.

Ray Cooksey and Richard Gates, two prominent management educators at the University of New England in Armidale, New South Wales, recently expressed a similar viewpoint when they stated that:

> ... [t]he focus of management education, therefore, should not be on case studies and current management literature, but on the study of domains such as literature, art, and aesthetic logic, which will assist managers recognise and utilise patterns of relationships.[17]

Without such a broadening of thinking in management education, explanations of organisational life and culture will continue to be linear and unrealistic. As we have seen throughout this book, the literature about story-telling and mythology clearly represents a slice of those mind- and spirit-expanding domains referred to by Cooksey and Gates. Studied from a story-telling perspective, organisational communication, behaviour, life and culture cannot be realistically understood from neat, linear flow-charts. The true picture of an organisation will more likely resemble a surrealistic collage, whose predominating themes are chaos and non-equilibrium.

Managers who have been caught up in the stimulating challenge of understanding the phenomenon of story-telling, however, may find it useful to seek out peers who are equally enthusiastic and interested. Informal groups made up of people like these could meet to raise issues, insights and problems for debate and discussion. Many of the topics of discussion are likely to be very practical. For example, a manager may want advice on why a memorandum-based story got the backs of the staff up or why a well-intentioned pep talk to a project team backfired because the story-line was misconstrued as criticism of the team's dedication and efforts to date.

Perhaps the most useful way to extend our learning and understanding of story-telling in organisations is to observe and concentrate attention on the stories other co-workers are communicating. As a first step in doing this, we need to remind ourselves that most communication between people in systems can be regarded as a form of story-telling. This point has already been emphasised in the earlier chapters of *Myth-makers and Story-tellers*. Once story-telling in organisations is acknowledged as a fact of life, our sense of curiosity will motivate us to listen actively to the stories of others. This will make us feel a part of the story-telling culture and life of the system in which we operate. Participant observation, however, is even more important for organisational development consultants, so we will turn our attention next to how they can be helped to understand an organisation's story-telling culture and use this understanding to recommend improvements to the system.

Consultants as story-tellers and story-listeners

Today's organisational development consultants are also referred to by other titles like 'change management specialists', 'communication or organisational auditors' and 'best practice consultants'. Each of these different titles suggests a particular functional focus or role. Auditors, for example, principally diagnose the state or health of the system. Best practice consultants offer advice on the most appropriate ways of managing an organisation. Change management specialists, on the other hand, do not only recommend the changes but also see to their implementation.

Avoiding pre-conceptions

Regardless of which of these roles they are enacting, consultants must guard themselves against the very natural temptation to understand any organisation only from their own or their clients' preconceptions.

The hidden agenda

When the story-telling of consultants is essentially intended to support a CEO's hidden reform agenda, only part of the organisation's realities is revealed. A few years ago, the Australian Commonwealth Government Department of Employment, Education and Training (DEET) commissioned a team of consultants attached to the National Centre for Vocational Education Research to review existing provisions for training vocational teachers. The consultants sought stories from a variety of stakeholders—current and graduated vocational learners, trainee and trained teachers, university-based teacher educators, officials from the teachers' union, bureaucrats from employers like state Departments of Technical and Further Education (TAFE) and human resource development representatives from relevant manufacturing companies such as BHP Steel.

At the time, the author was the head of a university school responsible for the professional education of vocational teachers and trainers. Consequently, he was approached by the consultants on several occasions to tell his story about the adequacy of current university provisions for vocational teacher education.

First he was interviewed for two hours and was asked through a series of both open-ended and specific questions to express his views about the effectiveness of the present system of university-based vocational teacher education. Next, he participated in a 'search conference' facilitated by these consultants. This get-together was made up of representatives of all the stakeholder groups. They were all asked to comment on the provision of vocational teacher education by universities. The author's third input came a few weeks later when he was invited to contribute to a national seminar, again facilitated by members of the consultant team.

> The search conference and the seminar created opportunities for shared story-telling both during the formal part of the events and the informal times between sessions or in the evenings. Two things became clear. Firstly, all of the participants spoke in glowing terms about the current university-based vocational teacher education courses. Secondly, all of the participants had a shared perception that the consultants were not being given the stories they wanted to hear. A great many of the stakeholders felt that DEET was being pressured by the managing directors of state TAFE systems to discredit the university vocational teacher education courses—because employers like TAFE were finding it too costly to put their teachers through professional development courses in universities. We assumed that this was the hidden agenda behind the audit and that the aim was to recommend the transfer of vocational teacher education from universities to centralised units within each state's TAFE system. One of the participants put the shared story-line very well when she said 'The consultants have already been given the conclusions to the report. What they want from us are the stories to justify those conclusions.'

It is often difficult for consultants to be truthful in their story-telling when the truth is the last thing an organisation's CEO wants to hear. So, one ability consultants need to cultivate is the crafting of truthful and accurate stories that are palatable and acceptable to those contracting their services. There is no blueprint for doing this successfully. Much will depend on whether the employer has an open mind, a genuine awareness of the stories being told in the organisation, faith in the story-telling ability of the consultant and a willingness to accept justifiable criticism should this be warranted. The reality is, unfortunately, that CEOs with these qualities are few and far between.

Essential skills for the consultant

Whether consultants are performing the role of diagnostician, of change agent, or of information resource, there are three abilities they should possess. These are the ability to:

- listen actively to the story of the person with the problem
- ask the right questions in the right sort of way
- offer alternative options or scenarios for resolving the problem.

These essential skills are all integral aspects of interpersonal communication competence.

Active listening

We have already seen that active listening necessitates being non-judgmental, empathy and skills in providing feedback. Consultants can lack these skills. Some consultants like to play the part of the guru. Despite appearing to listen intently to the story their contractor is telling, they may be saying to themselves, 'That poor clod doesn't know what the real problem is. This organisation needs an expert like me to put it straight.' When a consultant's listening is not only judgmental but also coupled with arrogance of this kind, there is a possibility that some inappropriate organisational changes will be recommended and even implemented.

Asking the right questions

Even mediocre external consultants usually don't come cheap, so it is important that relevant internal consultants or human resource management staff in organisations check out the story-telling and story-listening skills of the outsider they are thinking of contracting. The simplest way is to ask them to tell their story of how they would proceed to resolve either a hypothetical or real problem. What methods would they use to obtain all the necessary data for mapping the organisation? Whose stories would they ask to hear? How will they be able to determine if a story is true or a fabrication? What criteria would they use for generating recommendations for change?

> About a year ago, a relatively new university paid an external consultant a princely sum to undertake an audit of internal management practices. She interviewed, for about an hour at a time, every academic and administrative manager in the university. All heads of department and their executive superiors were involved in this exercise. Inevitably, the interviewees began to swap stories after the event. It soon became apparent that the consultant's frame of reference was biased from the very start. Most of the interviewed managers remembered being put on guard by the consultant's opening question: 'Which managers at this university, from the CEO down, do you think are falling down on their job?'.

Developing the art of story-telling

> Despite receiving assurances of anonymity and confidentiality, most of these managers felt uncomfortable and dodged giving the consultant direct answers or truthful stories. This consultant's problem was her assumption that something *had* to be wrong with the university's present management structure. It did not occur to her that the university may have been being managed quite satisfactorily at the time. The most off-putting thing about this consultant, however, was her insensitivity and lack of skill in questioning. When managers are bluntly asked by an unknown external consultant to disclose harmful stories about their peers and superiors they are bound to become suspicious and defensive. This is exactly what happened in the audit. Very little useful information was proferred by any of the interviewees. Twelve months down the track two new non-academic management positions were created in the university. The existing departments and divisions of the university remained unchanged.

What should this consultant have done instead? She would have done better to begin with a non-evaluative open-ended question like: 'Tell me about your managerial role in this organisation.' The interviewee would then have the option of being disclosive or evasive, without feeling any pressure to put down colleagues. Follow-up questions would also be less threatening if expressed positively. For instance, it would be preferable to be asked 'What kind of support do you need to get your job done?' and 'What kind of support are you getting?' rather than 'Which managers in this university are not giving you the support you need?'.

These differences are more than subtle. Injudicious wording can cause respondents to form negative attitudes and feelings towards the consultant. For consultants, questioning and listening are undoubtedly the two most important interpersonal communication skills they need to perform their roles in the story-telling organisation. These skills cannot be taken for granted as they sometimes are by certain consultants. In one organisation, all the executive staff were directed by the CEO to complete a managerial skills survey form designed by an external consultant. Few of the questions made any sense or seemed to apply to the respondents. They did not know how the questions had been dreamed up—certainly no one on the executive had been interviewed beforehand regarding the kind of work that they did.

Based on the confused responses, the report eventually came out and everyone received a copy. Every single manager received a job description that in all cases completely failed to match individual roles and responsibilities. *Some consultants prefer story-telling to story-listening.*

In reality, consultants do not have a choice. They need both kinds of skill to do their job properly. The art of story-telling and the skills of story-listening complement each other. They are two sides of one coin.

Generating change options

The third essential story-telling skill for consultants is the generation of options for change or resolving an organisational problem. This is a crucial skill which, in some instances, may be undervalued.

Reports and committees

In the past five years, the technical and further education (TAFE) system of New South Wales has been restructured twice. The earlier restructure was based on the recommendations of a committee of consultants led by Dr Brian Scott, whose report was popularly referred to as the 'Scott Report'. It was succinct, culminating in a specific set of recommendations without alternative possibilities. Shortly afterwards, many managerial positions were declared redundant and some very senior executives found themselves reporting to people who were once their subordinates.[18]

Those affected had hardly any time to get used to the changes and the new structure when a new managing director was appointed to the system. The first thing he did was to remodel TAFE all over again. Many more people became redundant or were offered temporary employment. This second wave of change seemed to put the idea into people's minds that the Scott Committee 'got the story all wrong'. Unfortunately, a great deal of damage had been done to numerous individuals and to the system before the organisation began to right itself. There is a good lesson here: never implement change hastily or simply on the basis of an expensive report from a team of consultants. Too often, organisations today have blind faith in the advice of consultants. This, of course, does not deny the fact that faith in reputable and highly credible consultants is often justified. What kind of provision can we make for consultants to develop these essential communication skills in the story-telling organisation? This is what we'll turn our attention to now.

Professional development for consultants

Because consultants need applied research skills, like the ability to diagnose organisational problems, much of these can be acquired through supervised practice in learning workshops. It is probably safe to assume that many successful consultants today have a university degree in behavioural sciences or a related field, and experience and training in organisational or human resource development. Consultants with this kind of background are most likely to be looking for training in the practicalities and techniques of organisational auditing. There are now many courses available on managing change in organisations.

Regardless of where the training may be provided, courses in organisational development or change management typically include a section on organisational problem diagnosis. The design of valid and reliable research procedures and instruments like survey forms, questionnaires, structured focus interviews and group problem-solving techniques usually constitutes an integral and core part of this type of training. It is very unlikely, however, that the art and skills of story-telling have been included in these training sessions—many of today's pragmatists would consider story-telling as something belonging to the world of 'play' or to the lunatic fringe of organisational behaviour theory rather than to what they see as the 'real world of work'.

Here's a curious point: some consultants who do not use the term 'story-telling' are actually enmeshed in the process. John McKenna, a consultant to a highly technical engineering organisation, says that one of the problems with the company's management was that:

> ... although they clearly saw the trees and could, from memory, tell you the details of every branch, the forest was a mystery to them.[19]

Most managers could not see the big picture and indicated that 'someone up the line' was taking care of the co-ordination of the activities of the various departments.

A familiar story? Among the interventions was the creation of departmental or 'natural work group' teams who were put through a training program for skill development in organisational diagnosis. One outcome of this training was that team members began to realise that they needed to communicate with people from other departments to really understand the organisation's problem. In essence, they were discovering that they only knew part of the story and that they needed to hear the stories of colleagues in other departments to get an accurate picture of organisation-wide as well as department-specific problems. Story-telling would have provided a powerful rationale for interventions in that consultancy.

Story-telling should not be considered as just another 'bag of tricks' to be added to the existing repertoire of consultant skills. It makes little sense to list story-telling as simply another auditing technique. Instruments like questionnaires or procedures like interviewing are all part of story-telling. They are the means for obtaining stories and for tapping into an organisation's mythology. Now that you have read a good deal about story-telling, can you imagine learning a sufficient amount of information about this powerful perspective in a short training session on organisational diagnosis? What would be the five or seven easy steps you would suggest for training participants to become experts in story-telling? It is plainly unhelpful to think in such terms.

Introducing consultants to story-telling

A training workshop on story-telling for consultants is really the foundation for lifelong self-directed learning. It can provide a broad conceptual framework for understanding and influencing organisational communication, life and culture. For this reason, the consultant's first exposure to the world of story-telling should be primarily an experience of excitement and wonderment—rather than of just acquiring new facts. Above all, the initial training workshop should not try to address too many new concepts or information superficially, but rather explore only those bits of information needed to grasp the general idea of what story-telling is. If done well, this preliminary experience of story-telling should whet the appetite of consultants and motivate them to learn more about this way of understanding organisational life.

Critical incident technique
The stories heard and told by participants in an initial consciousness-raising training session could be presented in a number of ways. For example, the 'critical incident technique' within a well developed simulation exercise could

be used to tell an official story about an organisational problem. The various participants could be assigned particular roles with accompanying instructions for the kinds of stories they would be telling. After all the stories are shared, the group of participants could have a discussion to determine the precise problem in the organisation and a set of options for resolving it. In addition to the training facilitator acting as an observer, it would be an advantage to have the entire simulation exercise video-recorded. By playing back the tape, participants could study the effectiveness of their story-telling and story-listening and make decisions about what they would do or say differently next time.

Alternative literature
After this taste of story-telling, perhaps the most valuable place to find out more about story-telling is in what Stephen Fineman and Yiannis Gabriel call 'alternative textbooks', which feature 'an empathy between the author and reader' and where learning occurs through 'serendipity'.[20] This contrasts with more conventional forms of learning resulting from suggestions by experts. Serendipity indicates not only that the learning is unexpected but also that the accidental discovery is 'pleasurable'. According to Fineman and Gabriel, today's alternative textbook writers all

> *... claim story-telling as the means of changing [organisational behaviour] teaching ... Instead of highlighting 'facts', they draw attention to feeling, meaning and experience.*[21]

Stories, then, are 'slices of life' and, in most cases, small-scale replicas of the organisation as a whole.

No doubt many consultants will find it strange to steep themselves in the alternative literature on story-telling. Equally, they will probably be more comfortable learning from conventional organisational behaviour textbooks that have simple, palatable and incontestable definitions of complex organisational phenomena, practical and 'real' rather than made-up case studies about organisational behaviour concepts like leadership or communication, and lists of information items. Boje and Dennehy have pointed to the futility of learning about organisational behaviour in these traditional ways. They

Part III: Building the story-telling organisation

see their task as a rebellion against contemporary management texts and to 'really provide life for business education'.[22] Furthermore, they comment that in conventional organisational behaviour education and training, all that participants are doing is '... memorising lists and playing non-sense exercises ... we will define lots of terms, but there is always more than one definition'.[23]

Another team of alternative textbook authors commented:

> [O]ur objective is to convey human experiences ... We believe that emotions play a central role in organisational dynamics, a role that has not been appreciated fully by organisational theorists.[24]

There is a popular belief in some organisations that 'consultants talk funny and make money'. As John March commented in an address to the Academy of Management:

> [C]onsulting is a substantial industry with substantial fees. The complaint, however, is less that they make money than the payments they receive are not warranted by the knowledge they provide ... They often seem to ignore—out of ignorance, laziness, or greed—relevant research literature ... They thrive on a diet of truisms, hyperbole and gimmicks. Any ideas they may have are lost in a terminology of salesmanship and a format of overconfidence.[25]

March goes on to say that consultants genuinely determined to understand accurately the communication and culture in organisations need to broaden their base for learning by finding new interpretations of experience in '... ideas, metaphors, models, and words that impose order on a confusing world, thus reconstructing our appreciation of experience'.[26]

There is a clear message here for consultants: understanding the complexities and realities of organisational life requires more comprehensive perspectives than those offered in conventional functionalist organisational behaviour texts. Story-telling provides one such perspective because 'stories are the cornerstone of the alternative textbook'.[27] For consultants, stories not only serve to provide insights into organisational events but they also can mirror accurately people's feelings and experiences which become symbols of the system's state of health. Eventually, sensitive and thoughtful consultants will become more and more competent at deconstructing the truth and lessons to be learned from an organisation's collection of stories and mythologies.

Summary

Our focus in this chapter has been on the professional development of managers and consultants as story-tellers. We have examined the kinds of story-telling roles they perform in organisations and the abilities they need to cultivate in order to carry out those roles effectively. It has been suggested that the training of managers-as-story-tellers should follow the 'learning by doing' approach involving practical experiential activities and be based on adult learning principles and goals.

With respect to the professional development of organisational development consultants, the creation of opportunities for serendipitous learning through alternative textbooks after the initial experience of consciousness-raising training has been strongly advocated.

We have also kept in mind the need for attitude change in managers and consultants as an essential first step to becoming competent story-tellers in organisations. For this attitude change to occur, it is suggested that managers and consultants broaden their thinking beyond traditional functionalist approaches to understanding organisational behaviour and focus on newer ways of interpreting communication and interpersonal experiences in human systems. In particular, the comments of several prominent contemporary management educators and organisational behaviour specialists have been cited to demonstrate the timeliness of adopting a story-telling rationale for understanding and analysing communication, culture and life in the workplace.

Our final chapter is an exploration of what the story-telling organisation will be like in the years that lie ahead and what kinds of competencies tomorrow's managers will need to have to be insightful and creative story-tellers. So, we have moved from learning about the myths of the past and how they have influenced our thinking today, to this point where we need to 'think smart' about the future. It will be an interesting and absorbing challenge.

7

organisational story-tellers of tomorrow

Things are more like they are now than they ever were before.
Dwight D. Eisenhower

If stories become the vehicle for understanding and changing organisational communication, behaviour and culture, how can people in systems capitalise on opportunities to be as expert as possible in story-telling? What kinds of advanced skills will they be able to develop? And what will the story-telling organisation of tomorrow be like? What changes can we expect to occur to the culture of the organisations in a few years' time? Will corporate and personal values change? Do we know if the external environment will continue to support the story-telling organisation? These are some of the intriguing questions we'll address in this final chapter.

The story-telling organisation of tomorrow

The story-telling organisation is only just finding its mark in the minds of today's sensitive, thinking managers, and there is a long way to go before our organisations are thought of by managers and consultants as rich sources of interpretive mythologies. According to Alvin Toffler, there are two contrasting ways in which people see the future. For most people, the future holds 'more of the same' despite a token acknowledgment that the times are a-changing. The other view of the future is that there probably will be no future because things seem to be getting worse day by day, as we are frequently reminded.[1]

Toffler regarded today's generation as 'the children of the next transformation, the Third Wave'. The First Wave occurred ten thousand years ago with the invention of agriculture and the Second Wave was heralded by the Industrial Revolution which commenced in the nineteenth century. While it is true that the Second Wave has not played itself out yet, a Third Wave is emerging and bringing with it 'a new age of synthesis'. There are important implications for how people will think about and view their private and professional worlds because there will be paradigmatic shifts in all intellectual fields. As Toffler has noted:

> *... from the hard sciences to sociology, psychology, and economics—especially economics—we are likely to see a return to large-scale thinking, to general theory, to the putting of the pieces back together again. For it is beginning to dawn on us that our obsessive emphasis on quantified detail without context, on progressively finer and finer measurement of smaller and smaller problems, leaves us knowing more and more about less and less.*[2]

Applied scholars and specialists committed to expanding their understanding of organisational communication and culture will inevitably move to using generic interdisciplinary organisational behaviour models which synthesise the thinking and concepts from a diversity of fields. There will be a shift from atomistic to holistic thinking. Whereas in Second Wave culture things are studied in isolation from one another, Third Wave culture focuses on *relationships* between things, the contexts in which those relationships can be understood, and the study of 'wholes' rather than bits.

If Toffler's vision is correct, organisations will be increasingly seen and accepted as theatres for story-telling, mythologising and the dramatisation of feelings and energies. The conception of the story-telling organisation as a venue for play-acting is intriguing. For one thing, we know there are many

Part III: Building the story-telling organisation

'plays' being performed simultaneously in an organisation's day to day life. There are plays about managing directors, union bosses, line managers, supervisors and rank-and-file members. Among the more common plots of these plays are power struggles between employers and employees, coalitions, conspiracies and intimate relationships between members of staff, the heroism of daring and courageous individuals, and the rise and fall of stars and supporting actors.

The story-telling organisation's theatre will also have producers and directors, dictating how the plays are to be acted out. Opinion leaders, at any level of the system, often direct actors' performances in particular, persuasive plays. Again, as plays rarely take place without sponsorship or support, the producers are likely to be those most committed to having the play's story told to any interested or supportive audience members in the system. The producers could thus be story-tellers with contrasting kinds of motives such as encouraging innovation and change, or, alternatively, destabilisation of the system through scandal-mongering. Sometimes, though not necessarily, the producers and directors may also be the scriptwriters. As we have seen, scriptwriters can be anyone in the system from the CEO down, or people like consultants not in the system but serving it.

Since each play has a limited number of actors, the audience consists of potentially every other non-playing member in the organisation. Prompters to remind players of their scripts and lines may stay behind the scenes in the shadow side. The designers of the set and props may provide a suitable context for the performance of the various story-plays. So, perhaps the main difference between the story-telling organisations of today and tomorrow will be that increasingly future generations will realise that they can learn many of the stories from daily 'live performances' by fellow actors in their systems. Organisational life will be seen as theatrical and system members will understand their available options of being either actors or spectators or both: remember Shakespeare's insightful words in *As You Like It*, 'All the world's a stage, and all the men and women merely players.'

In tomorrow's story-telling organisation, therefore, a corporate culture based on stories and myths will be the norm. But there will be exceptions. In a few years' time, some organisations will still prefer to remain as yesterday's organisations, deluded by the belief that any semblance of orderliness and efficiency is necessarily and sufficiently symptomatic of a healthy and productive system. These organisations will continue to look for linear, mechanistic solutions to non-linear, complex and messy problems. They will have had the opportunity to become a story-telling organisation but have chosen to use the simpler, more conventional pathway to self-understanding.

There will be only a very few of tomorrow's organisations ignoring the richness of their mythologies and denying their culture of story-telling. Most people are intelligent and motivated by exciting new ways of understanding their worlds, but the proliferation of vacuous how-to-do-it literature and training programs on management education suggests, more pessimistically and cynically perhaps, that the transition to Third Wave thinking—from familiar conceptualisations of organisations as complacent, sometimes moribund bureaucratic systems to bodies pulsating with life- and energy-giving stories—may be at least two decades away.

Story-telling competencies for tomorrow's managers

As people in systems increasingly come to regard story-telling as an inescapable reality of organisational life, they will start to think about developing additional higher order abilities. There are nine advanced competency areas that managers will need to have in the story-telling organisation of tomorrow. Managers will require abilities in:

- impromptu story-telling
- creative story-telling
- metaphorical thinking
- knowing the target audience
- enlisting audience involvement and participation
- co-producing through listening
- critical listening
- identifying mythical themes and the lessons to be learned from them
- applying new understandings and insights in helping the organisation and individuals to develop and change.

Impromptu story-telling

Impromptu story-telling is a spontaneous, unrehearsed form and may be likened to improvisation in jazz music. In jazz improvisation, there is a recognisable thematic structure. Although the tune is not played 'straight' but rather as a variation of the original melody line, key notes in each bar ensure that the improvisation is genuinely around a theme and that it is not just a random sequencing of sounds. This is an important point since the improvising jazz soloist is a member of a group whose collective sound must be harmonious and cohesive. As Ronald Purser and Alfonso Montuori have suggested,

> *... the jazz ensemble allows for a creative dialectic to exist between the individual and group. It is the uniqueness of the six different instruments in a jazz sextet that gives the ensemble its sound and mood; the absence or suppression of even one instrument would detract from the whole.*[3]

Similarly, artistic story-tellers of the future will be able to put together, with increasing ease and capability, a memorable, spontaneously woven story about a familiar topic, person, event or theme, while maintaining their interdependence with other story-tellers or co-producers in their organisations. In nations like the US today, many young people become articulate speakers because they are expected to undertake speech communication courses in senior high school or as university undergraduates. These courses encourage students to develop oral communication skills like public speaking.

Overcoming communication apprehension in public settings is one benefit students can gain from this kind of experience. As a result, their story-telling becomes more fluent and effortless. People who have a flair for impromptu speaking are often extraverted and sociable, enjoying having an audience to impress with their story-telling wit and artistry. Although, like jazz improvisation, impromptu story-telling does not always result in the production of new themes or plots, it requires creative ability in crafting an appealing narrative style that is capable of captivating the audience's attention.

Nevertheless, impromptu story-telling is not something of which only a gifted few are capable. With increasing practice, patience and a sincere desire to learn from each experience of story-telling, most people will relax and enjoy communicating with their listeners. When story-tellers conquer their apprehension and self-consciousness before audiences, they may also feel encouraged to write and tell their own original stories. These stories are 'new' in the sense that the interplay of people and events is probably very recent and known only to the story-tellers. Creative story-telling of this kind is the second area of competence the thinking managers of tomorrow will find it necessary and useful to develop.

Creative story-telling

As with impromptu story-telling, creative story-telling does not always entail the generation of original mythical themes. On the basis of our earlier explorations of organisational mythology, we can confidently conclude that the history of humankind has so far enabled story-tellers to appeciate that there is a limited number of themes about human relationships and that these themes have recurred over many centuries. This conclusion was reached over two thousand years ago by the preacher whose wisdom forms part of the *Holy Bible*'s *Old Testament*:

> *The thing that hath been, it is that which shall be; and that which is done, is that which shall be done; and there is no new thing under the sun.*[4]

Some of us will remember fine examples of creative story-telling in the BBC radio program 'My Word'. Frank Muir and Dennis Norden, the two story-tellers, would be asked to create stories around popular sayings or proverbs. Using amusing twists and embellishments, these master story-tellers would conclude each story with 'That's why . . .' followed by a comically altered and embellished version of the saying. For example, 'A rolling stone gathers no moss' might, as a result of the happenings in the story, end up as 'A reeling stern, galley's no mess'. In one very famous story, 'They can't take that away from me' was translated to 'Descartes, take that away from me!'

To think creatively, story-tellers need to find new ways of telling the same stories. This means seeing a person or an event from a different angle or perspective. In a three-dimensional model of the stucture of intellect, psychologist J. P. Guilford called creativity 'divergent thinking' and distinguished this from 'convergent thinking', which requires restricted or single solutions to problems.[5] A simple way to explain the difference between the two kinds of thinking can be shown by typical answers to a test of thinking styles. The 'Uses Test' requires respondents to list as many different uses as they can think of for a 'brick'. Convergent thinkers usually see bricks having one kind of use—building. Thus, their typical answers are 'For building a house' or 'For building a fireplace' or 'For building a wall'. Divergent or creative thinkers, on the other hand, see bricks being used, among other things, as door stops, weapons, paperweights, food (ice cream bricks) or for reducing the flow of water in cisterns.

Another psychology scholar, E. Paul Torrance, stated that 'showing relationships among apparently unrelated ideas' is an important feature of creativity.[6] This paralleled the development of a training approach known as 'synectics', whose goal was training people in creativity by requiring them to form relationships between diverse and often apparently irrelevant elements.[7] In the early 1960s, William J. J. Gordon founded the company Synectics Inc., which trained burnt-out executives from all kinds of organisations to think creatively again. Gordon and his colleagues would form training groups made up of architects, lawyers, engineers, marketing specialists, economists or representatives of any other profession. The important thing was to have people from different backgrounds learning together.

Each member of the training group would present an organisational problem needing a solution. The problem could be as basic as finding a new way of selling a product or as complex or sensitive as improving interpersonal communication and relationships in the organisation. Gordon's team of trainers encouraged the participants to use metaphors and analogies to make the strange familiar and the familiar strange. This process would unlock the participants from one-track thinking. What happened was that problem-owners gained new insights into how to deal with their problems by hearing their problems restated by fellow trainees working in unrelated professional fields.

It worked. There was a lot of shared story-telling where a new angle would be followed through to its denouement or climax. When the training was over, the participants were rejuvenated with fresh new ways of understanding and managing their organisational duties and problems. In short, they had become more creative in using others' stories to assist them in their professional life. The stories of others thus became metaphors for explaining and resolving real-life organisational issues and concerns.

Metaphorical thinking

Gordon's approach for training executives to be creative also draws our attention to the benefit of thinking in metaphors. In Chapter 4, we identified a range of metaphors people currently use when referring to their work or relationships with others in their organisations. The curious thing is that when the language of these metaphors becomes part of our normal vocabulary, we tend to forget we are thinking, acting and communicating in line with some symbolic image. The successful story-tellers of tomorrow will need, from time to time, to be able to 'detach' themselves from what they are doing and reflect on the metaphors which are currently guiding their story-telling.

Story-tellers who can be self-analytical in this way will have the advantage of either extending the present metaphor to create scope for new or improved stories or, of finding a different image to do this. Tomorrow's most capable story-tellers will also have the sensitivity to spot at once other people's metaphors and to evaluate fairly quickly the accuracy and applicability of those metaphors in their own organisation's mythologies. Some years ago, members of a college were reasonably content with their lot until an outsider referred to the place as 'an academic sweatbox'. This image put the idea into their heads that they were being expected to do much more than was reasonable in comparable higher education institutions elsewhere. What this suggests is that the metaphorical language we hear in others' stories can have a powerful influence on our own thinking and story-telling so long as our antennae remain sharply tuned in. Sensitivity to metaphor complements the ability to think in metaphor. Both abilities need to be cultivated by the successful story-tellers of tomorrow.

Knowing the target audience

There are probably other ingenious ways of helping people in systems tell the stories of their worklife more creatively. Tomorrow's managers need to find out about these and then try them out. No matter what technique they adopt to develop their creative story-telling powers, managers must make every effort to know their target audience. This means taking in all observable information to start with. It's a good idea for story-tellers to ask themselves a number of questions such as:

- How young and/or mature are the audience members?
- Are the audience members predominantly male or female?
- Is the audience multicultural or culturally homogeneous?
- Are the audience members superiors, subordinates or peers in the organisation?

Answers to these kinds of questions serve as useful initial reminders to story-tellers that their stories will be most effective if they are tailored to suit the characteristics of their audiences.

There are also questions story-tellers could be asking themselves while they are communicating their stories. Some of these may be:

- What audience member reactions indicate that the story is being well received or not?
- Is the story-listener paying attention?
- Is the story-listener showing signs of restlessness, impatience or lack of interest?
- Do any of the story-listeners give the impression that they have little or no idea of what I'm talking about?
- Does my story seem too convoluted or too complicated for them to follow?

Being aware of the audience's nature, needs and reactions helps the story-teller decide on some action or tactic to regain listeners' attention and involvement in the story. It is puzzling that young children's desire to participate in the story-telling process gradually disappears as they grow older. Most of us can recall the appealing look of wonderment in an infant's face as a parent points to pictures in a book while reading a story. We may also remember the child, hearing a story retold for the umpteenth time, becoming involved by pointing to the illustrations before the story-telling parent has had a chance to do so. Enthusiastic anticipatory responses like these seem to occur less frequently among adults.

Tomorrow's skilled story-tellers will explore and find diffferent ways of encouraging audience involvement. Regardless of how they achieve this, they will not expect their listeners to remain necessarily silent or passive. Story-telling will be more like a shared dialogue between the inspirer of the narrative and the audience members. Simple techniques such as asking listeners questions like 'And what do you think happened next?' or 'What would you have done if you had been X?' will become a natural part of the future story-teller's artistry and will help to keep the audience intrigued and engrossed.

Co-production

Perhaps the most intense kind of audience involvement will occur through co-production. Co-production may be regarded as a form of joint or group story-telling. The story unfolds as a result of audience members' prompts, additions and embellishments to the narrator's lead. Often the story can take an unusual twist or new direction because of a co-producer's intervention. The process is similar to an informal group sharing the telling of a 'shaggy dog story'. Individuals chip into the story-telling whenever they feel they have an entertaining or witty contribution to make. The skilled story-tellers of the future will have the ability not only to be a confident co-producer but also to inspire and help their listeners in the co-production of their stories.

To be good at co-producing, people need to be skilled listeners. Increasingly, today's managers are beginning to realise the importance of listening actively to what their staff have to say. The first thing a good listener must do is get the story-teller's story straight. Unfortunately, some managers seem to 'tune in and out' while others are telling their stories. Typically, the excuse they offer for this kind of half-listening is that they have many things to think about at the same time and thus cannot afford to ignore any of them. When managers delude themselves with this kind of thinking they carry out very few, if any, of their tasks efficiently. Even more importantly, they can lose the respect of those whose stories they attend to poorly. In turn, such loss of respect can destabilise and permanently damage crucial professional relationships.

Critical listening is another kind of story-telling ability tomorrow's managers need to cultivate.

Critical listening

Many of today's managers still use 'uncritical thinking' to make their decisions. This means they accept at face value and without question the stories others tell them. A major problem when this happens is that managers may only be hearing one side of a story while gullibly believing they have enough information to act. Critical listeners, on the other hand, do not put blind faith in the stories they hear but check out all the facts before deciding on how to proceed with a matter.

Being a critical listener does not mean always being a critic of the stories they hear and of the people who tell them. Rather, it involves evaluating the logic and validity of what a speaker has just said. This is not easy to do as we tend to be better at assessing the logic and validity of written stories than of spoken ones. There are, however, some good role models of critical thinking available to the story-telling manager. Adjudicators of debates, politicians, journalists, reporters and interviewers often find they have to 'think on their feet'. They rarely have the luxury of time and thoughtful preparation for responding to the stories they hear. Our story-listening managers of tomorrow cannot afford to be constantly duped by subordinates more competent in the art of story-telling. They will do well to learn to be critical listeners by imitating the example of relevant role models.

Identifying and interpreting mythical themes

Tomorrow's skilled story-listeners should also be able to identify the themes and lessons to be learned from the myths they encounter in their organisations. There is little point in being part of a story-telling culture if people remain completely unaffected by the stories they share. It is only natural for us to be moved by heroic deeds, courageous and humane behaviours or by someone's selfless support of colleagues. Equally, we are easily disillusioned or dismayed by antisocial actions and destructive story-telling. In each case, there is something we can learn, regardless of whether this may be what or what not to do next time. For this reason, the best story-tellers are always delving deeply into the stories coming to them, so that they can create new insights and meanings about their personal and organisational worlds.

Some of the stories we hear may be immortalised on tape or transcribed into print. This often happens with keynote addresses or prize winning papers at conferences, for example. Our parliaments, local municipal councils and courts of law keep detailed records of any public proceedings. All companies keep records of annual general meetings. More commonly, on a day-to-day basis, we receive recorded stories in memoranda, letters, recorded telephone messages or on electronic mail.

With records like these, people have the opportunity to replay or re-read stories and thus to form deeper understandings about their themes and lessons. Such insightful meanings are part of an inner dialogue or, if you like, 'self-talk' which involves the reworking of stories by their receiver(s). Roman Jakobson in defining the 'two cardinal and complementary traits of verbal behavior' stated that:

> *... inner speech is in its essence a dialogue, and that any reported speech is appropriated and remolded by the quoter, whether it is a quotation from an alter or from an earlier phase of the ego.*[8]

Ability to learn from self-talk, therefore, will be an important characteristic of future story-tellers. It will require a lot of concentration, effort and focused commitment on the part of busy managers wanting to contribute constructively to their story-telling organisations.

Applying new insights

This brings us to the ninth ability tomorrow's story-tellers will need to have—the capacity to apply their newly acquired understandings and insights to help people in systems develop and change. Perhaps this will be the hardest of all things for story-telling managers to do. In a sense, the ability to apply new learnings depends on the possession of the other abilities like thinking creatively through metaphors. The point, however, is this: there is little reason for a story-telling organisation if its stories and mythologies are ignored as essential databases and beacons for change.

One of the main differences between the organisations of tomorrow and those of yesterday is that people will increasingly realise that story-sharing obviates a good deal of conflict and correspondingly optimises the probability of consensus for change and innovation. Just as in many of today's organisations change typically occurs through executive edicts or proclamations, in tomorrow's story-telling organisations change will more frequently occur through involving as many members as possible in open communication and team dialogue. Of course, there may be obstacles managers will have to circumvent in their quest for story-telling competence, so we'll give these some thought in the following section.

Monitoring cultural change and differences

A few years from now, managers determined to operate successfully in their story-telling organisations will need to be aware of the changing cultural forces, within and outside them, which could have a bearing on their development as myth interpreters and story-tellers.

Cultural changes could occur at any of three levels:

- within the individual
- within the system or organisation
- outside of the system.

If managers fail to register that changes are happening within themselves and the environment in which they work, their stories will appear irrelevant and have little impact on target audiences. So, how do we think managers will need to be different in tomorrow's story-telling organisation?

At the personal or individual level, managers will need to re-examine their beliefs, attitudes and values. One very probable change is towards managers placing greater value on their communication and relationships with their staff. Correspondingly, there is likely to be less importance attached to the 'mechanics of management' or the daily grind of administrative busywork. Management will be seen more and more as a process of helping staff in their work and managers will realise that story-telling and story-listening are critical competencies for doing this. The notion of manager-as-boss will be replaced by the increasingly more accepted view of manager-as-facilitator-of-change through frequent open communication with staff members. Many of us recognise this as a shift to becoming 'transformative managers' who value shared story-telling and good relationships with their staff and who believe in spending a lot of time listening to them and providing professional and emotional support.[9]

Tomorrow's managers will need to understand, as many of today's managers remain determined not to understand, that listening to the stories of their staff is vital for identifying staff members' needs and for deciding upon ways of addressing those needs. Story-telling will be seen as a *sine qua non* for maintaining a healthy quality of life in organisations. This is not limited to the manager's specific piece of turf.

As organisations become more complex, their survival depends on information from increasing numbers of specialists like taxation experts, lawyers and investment advisers. Alvin Toffler calls these the 'business commandos' of modern organisations and argues that managers are becoming more and more dependent on these specialists' stories. Knowledge, Toffler says, is 'a key weapon in the power struggles that accompany the emergence of the super-symbolic economy'.[10]

So, managers need to listen not only to the stories of people with whom they work most closely but also to those of others in and beyond their organisations. To do this they will need a 'story-listening radar' which keeps track of all that is going on around them. For their own survival managers will need to activate their radars particularly when they suspect shadow side story-telling in their workplaces. By knowing the stories in circulation, managers can keep pace with current thinking in their organisations and can even be one step ahead in preparing for likely changes. With sensitive radar equipment, tomorrow's managers in the story-telling organisation will thus be less susceptible to unexpected shocks or calamities than many of today's managers still appear to be.

Some of the signs of change to the workplace in future years are with us now. For one thing, today's organisations are becoming increasingly multicultural. Witness places like Australia's Gold Coast and America's Honolulu, where nearly every story is told in two languages—English and Japanese. Tomorrow's story-telling managers, therefore, will need to be sensitive to cultural differences, in expectations of men versus women at work, and in formal communication and etiquette, among other things.

While managers will continue their policies and practices of being even-handed to all their staff, they will need to understand the subtle nuances which differentiate ways of showing respect or disrespect from one culture to another. For example, the familiarity used by some male Anglo-Australian managers when greeting their staff may be insulting to people of different ethnic origins. It is highly improbable that expressions like 'How are you doing, you old bugger?' will be well received or understood as intended by people from cultures where words like bugger have only a denotatively derogatory meaning.

There is nearly always a problem with translating literally from one language to another. Here are some examples:

- an American food chain, Taco Times Restaurants, had to change its name when moving into the Japanese market because 'taco' means 'idiot' in Japanese
- Mitsubishi Pajero had a lukewarm reception in South American countries because its slogan 'Have an affair with a Pajero' translated into certain local dialects meant 'Have an affair with a gay'
- the famous Pepsi-cola slogan 'Come alive with Pepsi' translated into German as 'Come out of the grave' and in Taiwan as 'bring your ancestors back from the dead'
- General Motors' 'Body by Fisher' became 'Corpse by Fisher' in Flemish and its automobile, the 'Nova', literally means 'It doesn't go' in Spanish
- the Spanish literal translation for 'Let Hertz put you in the driver's seat' was 'Let Hertz make you a chauffeur'
- Braniff's 747 'Rendezvous Lounge' translates into Portuguese as Braniff's 747 'Meet Your Mistress Lounge'.[11]

By developing sensitivity and competence in intercultural communication, tomorrow's managers will increase the chances of having their stories favourably received by their co-workers.

Preparing to 'buck the system'

It will not be enough, however, for managers to keep informed about all the stories within their organisations. The astute managers of the future will also use their radar to monitor developments, changes and current thinking in the external environment. This means that 'the way we do things around here' will not be the only or major guiding work principle for tomorrow's managers in the story-telling organisation. If the stories these managers hear from the world outside their organisations point to the need for changes to the system, two choices will be available—either to 'back the system' or to 'buck the system'.

Managers who back their systems tend to be preservers of the status quo. To them, change is disruptive and leads to deterioration in staff morale. By backing the present way of doing things, they devote their energies to finding reasons or evidence for not changing. Their motto is 'when you're on a good thing, stick to it'. Take the case of a recent downsizing exercise in one of Australia's leading life assurance companies.

> Eight highly regarded currently employed managers were competing for three positions after five positions had been declared redundant. A team of organisational development consultants administered a battery of aptitude tests to the eight applicants. The scores were benchmarked against top scores of managers from America's five leading organisations.
>
> One of the eight managers scored so highly that the consultants reported to the CEO her ability to lead an organisation like any one of the top American five. The CEO then did something strange—he asked the manager to return to him her copy of the consultants' report. He gave the reason that her score was 'too high' and that the test results would be adjusted according to internal company standards which in his view were more rigorous than the standards in America's top five companies. It is easy to see that this CEO was a system backer. He was not prepared to hear the consultants' story because it did not match up with his preconceived conclusions and intentions.

By contrast, managers who are not afraid to 'buck their systems' are prepared to take risks and are committed to stand by their principles. In conservative organisations, managers who have been known to buck the system are usually regarded as mavericks because they always appear to 'go it alone' rather than to 'do it the company way'. They listen to everyone's stories in order to get the 'big picture'. Rarely are they applauded for any change at the time it is implemented but may be given credit for this innovation years later when those affected are more relaxed about things. Managers who buck the system when they see the need for change follow the motto *'carpe diem'* which, translated, means 'seize the day'. Such opportunities become more abundant when managers listen to all the stories of people in and outside of their organisations. Tomorrow's story-telling managers will be like that.

Summary

In this chapter we've caught a glimpse of what the future story-telling organisation will be like and of the kinds of communicative abilities managers will need to have in order to contribute creatively, constructively and successfully to the life and work of their organisations. We have also seen how important it will be for tomorrow's managers to seize every opportunity to learn from the stories that circulate within and outside of their organisations.

Our brief look into the future should give us a feeling of optimism about tomorrow's managers. Such optimism will be justified if managers are prepared to accept the legitimacy, practicality and usefulness of the story-telling perspective. Because stories are the breath of life in organisations, managers who want to learn and develop through story-telling and story-listening will find their professional worlds more intelligible and satisfying. Let's hope that the majority of tomorrow's managers will find their story-telling organisation stimulating, exciting and engrossing.

We have come to the end of this part of our journey into the world of story-telling. So, where to from here? Has this journey enticed you to find out even more about the stories and myths which help you stay in touch with all that is significant in your world of work? It's now up to you to tap into the story-telling culture of your organisation and to enrich your experience of your professional life. If you are continuing this journey, I wish you well.

Endnotes

Chapter 1

1. Blanchard, K. & Johnson, S. (1983) *The One Minute Manager*, Sydney: Collins.
2. Schank, R. C. (1990) *Tell Me a Story: A New Look at Real and Artificial Memory*, New York: Charles Scribner's Sons, Macmillan, pp. 40–53.
3. Campbell, J. & Moyers, B. (1988) *The Power of Myth*, New York: Doubleday, p. 4.
4. McCullagh, C. (1994) 'Two Dead Cats, the Alfalfa on the Carpet, and Other Urban Myths', *Good Weekend: The Sydney Morning Herald Magazine*, 3 September, 38–40.
5. Egan, G. (1993) *Adding Value: A Systematic Guide to Business-Driven Management and Leadership*, San Francisco: Jossey-Bass.
6. Peter, L. J. (1986) *Why Things Go Wrong or the Peter Principle Revisited*, London: Unwin, p. 117.

Chapter 2

1. Boje, D. M. (1991) 'Consulting and Change in the Storytelling Organisation', *Journal of Organizational Change Management*, 4, 8.
2. Egan, G. (1988) *Change Agent Skills A: Assessing and Designing Excellence*, San Diego: University Associates, 157.
3. Vance, C. M. (1991) 'Formalising Storytelling in Organisations: A Key Agenda for the Design of Training', *Journal of Organizational Change Management*, 4, 52.

4. Van Buskirk, W. & McGrath, D. (1992) 'Organizational Stories as a Window on Affect in Organizations', *Journal of Organizational Change Management*, 5, 12.
5. Senge, P. M. (1994) *The Fifth Discipline: The Art and Practice of the Learning Organization*, Sydney: Random House Australia.
6. Kaye, M. (1994) *Communication Management*, Sydney: Prentice Hall.
7. Bennis, W. (1991) *Why Leaders Can't Lead: The Unconscious Conspiracy Continues*, San Francisco: Jossey-Bass, p. 18.
8. Peters, T. (1989) *Thriving on Chaos: Handbook for a Management Revolution*, London: Pan, pp. 425–6.
9. Roberts, W. (1993) *Victory Secrets of Attila the Hun*, London: Bantam, p. 51.
10. Bennis, *op. cit.*, pp. 20–1.
11. Wolvin, A. & Coakley, C. (1988) *Listening* (3rd edn), Dubuque: Brown, p. 283.
12. Senge, *op. cit.*, pp. 13–14.

Chapter 3

1. Frye, N. (1968) 'New Directions from Old', in (ed.) H. A. Murray, *Myth and Mythmaking*, Boston: Beacon Press, pp. 114–31.
2. Campbell, J. & Moyers, B. (1988) *The Power of Myth*, New York: Doubleday, p. 31.
3. Lonergan, J. (1994) 'Paradigm People: New Leaders for the Chaos Decade', *Management*, May, pp. 34–6.
4. Boje, D. M., Fedor, D. B. & Rowland, K. M. (1982) 'Myth-making: A Qualitative Step in OD Interventions', *Journal of Applied Behavioral Science*, 18, 24.
5. Bellingham, R. & Cohen, B. (1989) *Leadership—Myths and Realities*, Amherst: Human Resource Development Press, p. 114.
6. Campbell, J. (1969) *The Flight of the Wild Gander: Explorations in the Mythical Dimension*, Chicago: Regnery Gateway, p. 17.
7. Barthes, R. (1993) *Mythologies*, London: Vintage, p. 157.

Chapter 4

1. Kluckhohn, C. (1968) 'Recurrent Themes in Myths and Mythmaking', in (ed.) H. A. Murray, *Myth and Mythmaking*, Boston: Beacon Press, pp. 46–60.
2. Boje, D. M. (1994) 'Organizational Storytelling: The Struggles of Pre-modern, Modern and Postmodern Organizational Discourses', *Management Learning*, 25, 433–62.

Endnotes

3. Craig, J. (1994) 'Stories, Myths and Archetypes—An Alternative Approach to Organizational Culture', in (eds) Kaye, M. & Saunders, S. 'Monograph Series: Communication in Vocational Education and Training', Sydney: University of Technology, Sydney, p. 132.
4. Cotterell, A. (1992) *A Dictionary of World Mythology*, Oxford: Oxford University Press, p. 53.
5. Roberts, W. (1993) *Victory Secrets of Attila the Hun*, London: Bantam, p. 42.
6. Tennyson, A. L. (1906) *The Works of Alfred Lord Tennyson*, London: Macmillan, p. 473.
7. 'Gospel of St Matthew', 4: 1–11, in (1975) *The Holy Bible*, King James Version, Nashville: Thomas Nelson.
8. For example, Deut. 32: 35; Psalm 58: 10; Isaiah 34: 8; Jerem. 11: 20.
9. Martin, J., Feldman, M. S., Hatch, M. J. & Sitkin, S. B. (1983) 'The Uniqueness Paradox in Organizational Stories', *Administrative Science Quarterly*, 28, 438–53.
10. Jung, C. G., von Franz, M.-L., Henderson, J. L., Jacobi, J. & Jaffe, A. (1983) *Man and His Symbols*, New York: Doubleday, p. 67.
11. *Ibid.*, p. 73.
12. Bird, B. J. (1992) 'The Roman God Mercury: An Entrepreneurial Archetype', *Journal of Management Inquiry*, 1, 205–12.
13. McGregor, D. (1960) 'Theory X and Theory Y', in (ed.) D. S. Pugh, *Organization Theory: Selected Readings*, London: Penguin, 1990, p. 358.
14. Herzberg, F. (1966) 'The Motivation-Hygiene Theory', in Pugh, *ibid.*, p. 379.
15. Gen. 3: 12.
16. Hequet, M. (1992) 'Poof! Myth and Fable Appear as Human Development Tools', *Training*, 29, 48.
17. Campbell, J. (1973) *The Hero with a Thousand Faces*, Princeton: Princeton University Press.
18. Spreitzer, G. M., Quinn, R. E. & Fletcher, J. (1995) 'Excavating the Paths of Meaning, Renewal, and Empowerment: A Typology of Managerial High-Performance Myths', *Journal of Management Inquiry*, 4, 16–39.
19. Shakespeare, William, *Henry V*, act 4, scene 3.

Chapter 5

1. Peters, T. J. & Waterman, R. H. (1984) *In Search of Excellence: Lessons from America's Best-Run Companies*, Sydney: Harper & Row, p. 75.

Endnotes

2. McMurray, A. J. (1994) 'The Relationship Between Organizational Culture and Organizational Climate with Reference to a University Setting', paper presented to the Joint International Communication Association/Australian and New Zealand Communication Association Conference, Sydney Convention and Exhibition Centre and University of Technology, Sydney, 11–15 July 1994, p. 2.
3. Goldhaber, G. M. (1993) *Organizational Communication*, (6th edn) Madison, Wisconsin: WCB Brown & Benchmark, p. 69.
4. Schein, E. H. (1992) *Organizational Culture and Leadership: A Dynamic View* (2nd edn) San Francisco: Jossey-Bass.
5. Sackmann, S. A. (1991) 'Uncovering Culture in Organizations', *Journal of Applied Behavioral Science*, 27, 295–317.
6. Hofstede, G. (1980) 'Motivation, Leadership and Organization: Do American Theories Apply Abroad', in (ed.) D. S. Pugh *Organization Theory: Selected Readings*, London: Penguin, 1990, p. 475.
7. Ouchi, W. (1981) 'Going from A to Z: Thirteen Steps to a Theory Z Organization', *Management Review*, 70: 8–16.
8. Irwin, H. & More, E. (1994) *Managing Corporate Communication*, Sydney: Allen & Unwin, p. 19.
9. Deal, T. & Kennedy, A. (1982) *Corporate Cultures: The Rites and Rituals of Corporate Life*, Reading, Massachusetts: Addison-Wesley.
10. Pacanowsky, M. E. & O'Donnell-Trujillo, N. (1982) 'Communication and Organizational Cultures', *Western Journal of Speech and Communication*, 46: 115–130.
11. Duck, J. D. (1993) 'Managing Change: The Art of Balancing', *Harvard Business Review*, November–December, 110.
12. Jensen, A. D. & Chilberg, J. C. (1991) *Small Group Communication: Theory and Application*, Belmont, California: Wadsworth, p. 378.
13. Bormann, E. G. (1983) 'Symbolic Convergence: Organizational Communication and Culture', in (eds) L. L. Putnam & M. E. Pacanowsky, *Communication and Organizations: An Interpretive Approach*, Newbury Park, California: Sage, p. 113.
14. Hames, R. D. (1994) *The Management Myth: Exploring the Essence of Future Organisations*, Sydney: Business & Professional Publishing, pp. 4–6.
15. Hackman, M. Z. & Johnson, C. E. (1991) *Leadership: A Communication Perspective*, Prospect Heights, Illinois: Waveland Press, pp. 145–6.
16. Peters, T. (1989) *Thriving on Chaos: Handbook for a Management Revolution*, London: Pan, p. 418.

17. Egan, G. (1993) *Adding Value: A Systematic Guide to Business-Driven Management and Leadership*, San Francisco: Jossey-Bass, p. 91.
18. *Ibid.*, p. 92.
19. Tichy, N. M. (1983) *Managing Strategic Change: Technical, Political and Cultural Dynamics*, New York: John Wiley & Sons, p. 131.
20. Postman, N. & Weingartner, C. (1972) *Teaching as a Subversive Activity*, Harmondsworth, England: Penguin, p. 16.
21. Gilpin, A. (1995) 'Organisational Viruses: An Analogy for Understanding Organisational Performance', unpublished MBA thesis, University of New England.
22. Egan, *op. cit.*, pp. 113–19.

Chapter 6

1. Sydney Adventist Hospital Public Relations Department (1994) 'What YOU should know about Sydney Adventist Hospital', Sydney: Sydney Adventist Hospital, p. 3.
2. Bass, B. (1988) 'The Inspirational Processes of Leadership', *Journal of Management Development*, 7, 21–31.
3. Atwater, L., Penn, R. & Rucker, L. (1991) 'Personal Qualities of Charismatic Leaders', *Leadership and Organization Development Journal*, 12, 7–10.
4. *Ibid.*, 10.
5. *Ibid.*
6. Bass, *op. cit.*, 22.
7. Tichy, N. & Devanna, M. A. (1985) *Transformational Leadership*, New York: Wiley, p. 94.
8. Weick, K. (1979) 'Cognitive Process in Organizations', in (ed.) B. Shaw, *Research in Organizational Behavior*, Vol. 1, Greenwich: JAI Press.
9. Hunt, J. G., Baliga, B. R. & Peterson, M. F. (1988) 'Strategic Apex Leader Scripts and an Organisational Life Cycle Approach to Leadership and Excellence', *Journal of Management Development*, 7, 71.
10. Bell, C. R. & Margolis, F. H. (1989) 'The Practice of Training: A Matter of Perspective', *Journal of Management Development*, 8, 43.
11. Snell, R. (1989) 'Graduating from the School of Hard Knocks?', *Journal of Management Development*, 8, 24.
12. Finlay, M. & Hogan, C. (1994) 'Who Will Bell the Cat? Story Telling Techniques for People who Work with People in Organisations', a paper presented at

Endnotes

the Third International Organizational Behaviour Teaching Conference, University of Otago, Dunedin, New Zealand, 14–17 December 1994, pp. 15–16.
[13] Rifkin, W. D. (1994) 'Twenty-five Ways to Spot an Expert', Department of Management, University of Wollongong, one page mimeograph.
[14] Culley, H. C. (1989) 'Overcoming Resistance to Management Development', *Journal of Management Development*, 8, 5–6.
[15] *Ibid.*, 5.
[16] Savery, L. K. (1988) 'Comparison of Managerial and Non-managerial Employees' Desired and Perceived Motivators and Job Satisfaction Levels', *Leadership and Organization Development Journal*, 9, 19.
[17] Cooksey, R. W. & Gates, G. R. (1994) 'HRM: A Management Science in Need of Discipline', *Journal of the Australian and New Zealand Academy of Management*, 1, 2.
[18] Kaye, M. (1994) 'Implementing Change in Australian Tertiary Education Systems: Reflections on Some Practical Strategies', *Unicorn*, 20, 53–4.
[19] McKenna, J. F. & Yeider, R. A. (1991) 'Management Development for an Organisation in Transition', *Journal of Management Development*, 10, 58.
[20] Fineman, S. & Gabriel, Y. (1994) 'Paradigms of Organizations: An Exploration in Textbook Rhetorics', *Organization*, 1, 389.
[21] *Ibid.*, 390.
[22] Boje, D.M. & Dennehy, R.F. (1993) *Managing in the Postmodern World*, Dubuque: Kendall/Hunt, pp. xxvi–xxviii.
[23] *Ibid.*, pp. xxvi–xxviii.
[24] Frost, P. J., Mitchell, V. F. & Nord, W. R. (eds) (1992) *Organizational Reality: Reports from the Firing Line* (4th edn) New York: Harper Collins, pp. ix–x.
[25] March, J. G. (1991) 'Organizational Consultants and Organizational Research', *Journal of Applied Communication Research*, 19, 22.
[26] *Ibid.*, 29.
[27] Fineman & Gabriel, *op. cit.*, 390.

Chapter 7

[1] Toffler, A. (1980) *The Third Wave*, London: Pan, p. 25.
[2] *Ibid.*, p. 142.
[3] Purser, R. E. and Montuori, A. (1994) 'Miles Davis in the Classroom: Using the Jazz Ensemble Metaphor for Enhancing Team Learning', *Journal of Management Education*, 18, 22.
[4] Eccles. 1: 9.

Endnotes

5. Guilford, J. P. (1959) 'Traits of Creativity', in (ed.) P. E. Vernon, *Creativity*, Harmondsworth: Penguin, pp. 179–80.
6. Torrance, E. P. (1967) 'Nurture of Creative Talents', in (eds) G. A. Davis & J. A. Scott, *Training Creative Thinking*, New York: Holt, Rinehart & Winston, 1971, p. 213.
7. Gordon, W. J. J. (1961) 'Synectics', in (eds) Davis & Scott, *op. cit.*, pp. 14–29.
8. Jakobson, R. (1964) 'Language in Operation', cited in C. Ginzburg (1990) *Myths, Emblems, Clues*, London: Hutchinson Radius, p. 159.
9. Dunphy, D. & Stace, D. (1990) *Under New Management: Australian Organizations in Transition*, Sydney: McGraw-Hill, p. 163.
10. Toffler, A. (1991) *Power Shift: Knowledge, Wealth, and Violence at the Edge of the 21st Century*, New York: Bantam, p. 25.
11. Saee, J. & Kaye, M. (1994) 'Intercultural Communication Competence in Management Training with Reference to Australian Organizations', paper presented to the Joint International Communication Association/Australian and New Zealand Communication Association Conference, Darling Harbour and University of Technology, Sydney, 11–14 July, pp. 6–7.

Index

Abel, 81
Abraham, 83, 88
active listening, 162
acts of God (*see also* disasters), 78–9
Adam, 84, 87–8
adult learning principles and goals, 154–7
Aegeus, 54
Aida, 57
Alessi, 92
Alexander the Great, 95, 102
Alien, 92
allegory, 88
alternative textbooks, 167–8
Anderson, Hans Christian, 5
Androcles, 95
Apocalypse Now, 96
Apple Macintosh, 73, 124
arationality, 127–9, 142
archetypes, 76, 86–91, 104, 135
Ariadne, 54, 55
Attica, 53–4
Attila the Hun, 35, 82
Atwater, Leanne, 142–3
audience, 17–18, 21, 37, 97, 151, 172, 173, 177–9
audience involvement, 42–5, 173
Australia Post, 115

Australian Broadcasting Commission, 99
AV Jennings Homes, 77

Baird, John Logie, 94
Baliga, B. R., 144
Barnard, Christian, 94
Barthes, Roland, 68
Bass, Bernard, 142–3
Batman, 91
Becker, Boris, 92
Bell, Chip, 147
Bellingham, R., 65
Bennis, Warren, 35, 36
best practice, 6, 159
Bible, The, 77, 78, 81, 83, 84, 87–8, 103, 175
Bird, Barbara J., 86–7
Blaise, Modesty, 91
Blanchard, Kenneth, 6
Boadicea, 90
Body Shop, The (*see also* Roddick, Anita), 89
Boje, David, 23, 61, 76, 167–8
Bond, Alan, 62
Borg, Bjorn, 92
Bormann, Ernest G., 120
Bradley, Gen. Omar Nelson, 95

Index

Braniff Airways, 184
bucking the system, 184–6
Budget Rent-A-Car, 65–6
Buffett, Warren, 92
Bukowski, Charles, 94
Bumstead, Blondie, 91
business commandos, 183

Caesar, Julius, 95, 102
Cain, 81
Campbell, Joseph, 3, 55, 67, 95–7
case study, 6
Castro, Fidel, 126
Cawley, Evonne, 92
Ceres (*see also* Demeter, earth mother), 89
Chamberlain, Lindy, 96
change management specialists, 159–60
   generating change options, 164
changing cultural forces in organisations, 26–7, 61, 182–4
charisma, 18
charismatic leaders, 111, 142
Chilberg, Joseph C., 118
Christie, Agatha, 92
Chrysler (US) Motor Corporation, 60
Churchill, Winston, 126
Clinton, Bill, 99
Coakley, C., 45
Cohen, B., 65
Colman, Arthur, 91
Columbus, Christopher, 68
communication, 4–5, 17, 22, 23, 25–6, 30, 33–6, 100, 108, 120, 123, 125, 153, 156–9, 164, 166, 169, 171, 174–5, 177–8, 182
   apprehension, 174
   auditors (*see also* organisational auditors), 159
   competence, 39, 48, 184, 186
   open, 30, 108, 124, 182
communicative goals, 6–7

competence, 18, 42, 48, 138, 156, 169
conflict resolution, 139, 141–2
constructs, 116
convergent thinking, 175–6
conversational goals, 6–7
Cook, Capt. James, 68
Cooksey, Ray, 158
co-production of stories (co-story-telling), 43, 173, 179
Cornwell, Patricia, 92
Cotterell, Arthur, 79
Court, Margaret, 92
Crete, 53–4, 74
Craig, John, 77
creative story-telling, 173, 175–7
credibility, 10, 13, 16–18, 38, 45, 84, 145
critical incident technique, 166–7
critical listening, 45, 173, 179–80
cross-cultural influences, 110
Culley, Henry C., 153–4
culture myth, 112
Curie, Marie and Pierre, 94

David Jones, 65–6
Deal, Terrence E., 116
De Gama, Vasco, 68
De Gaulle, Gen. Charles, 102
Demeter (*see also* Ceres, earth mother), 89
Deming, W. Edward, 110
demythologising our world, 61, 68, 123
Dennehy, R. F., 167–8
Department of Employment, Education and Training (DEET), 160–1
Deucalion, 78, 90
Devanna, Mary Anne, 143
Dionysus, 90
Dirty Harry Callahan, 92
disasters (*see also* acts of God), 78–9
discourse, 76
divergent thinking, 175–6
Donovan, Jason, 58

Index

dragon-slaying (*see also* monster-slaying), 54, 74, 79
Duck, Jeanie Daniel, 117
Dunphy, Dexter, 183
dynamism, 18

Earheart, Amelia, 94
earth mother (*see also* Ceres, Demeter), 89
Echo, 84
Edison, Thomas Alva, 94
Egan, Gerard, 15–16, 23, 99, 126–7, 133
einherjar, 97
Eisenhower, Gen. Dwight D., 95
emotive language, 17–18, 37
empathy (*see also* story-listening), 46–7, 49
entrepreneur
    Mercury as archetype, 86–7
entropy, 24, 78
epics, 12, 57, 73, 74
Esau, 81
Eskimo story-tellers, 56
Eurydice, 84
Eve, 84, 87–8
Evert, Chris, 92
expertise, 18

facts, 116
fantasy-based stories (*see also* stories), 57
    themes, 120–2, 131, 144
    types, 121–2, 131
Faust, 84
fear appeals, 18
Fedor, Donald B., 61
feedback (*see also* story-listening), 47–8, 49
Feldman, Martha S., 86
Fineman, Stephen, 167–8
Finlay, Marie, 149–51
Fleming, Alexander, 94
Fleming, Ian, 92

Fletcher, Jerry, 96
Flood, The Great, 77–8, 90
Frost, P. J., 168
Frye, Northrop, 55

Gabriel, Yiannis, 167–8
Gagarin, Yuri, 94
Gandhi, Mahatma, 96
Gates, Bill, 58
Gates, G. Richard, 158
General Electric, 73
General Motors, 184
Gilgamesh, epic of, 78
Gilpin, Anne, 132
gods, 31, 59, 74
Goldhaber, Gerald M., 108
Gordon, William J. J., 176–7
    synectics, 176–7
gossip, 9–10, 38
Grimm, Brothers, 5
Grim Reaper advertisement, 18
Guilford, J. P., 175–6

Hackman, Michael, 125
Hades, 89
Hames, Richard, 123–4
Hannibal, 95, 102
Harrods, 58
Hatch, Mary Jo, 86
Hemmingway, Ernest, 132
Henderson, J. L., 86
Hequet, Marc, 91
Hera, 84
Hercules, 74, 90
heroes, 10, 54, 68, 73, 74, 76, 78, 81–3, 85, 86, 91–7, 104, 135, 142, 180
    anti-heroes, 73, 85
    as role-models, 92–5, 104
    comic book, 57, 91–2
    detective, 92
    'generic' heroes, 92–5

Index

heroes—*cont'd*
   hero's journey, 95–7
   movie, 92
   sporting, 92, 93
Hertz car rental, 184
Herzberg, Frederick, 88
Heyerdahl, Thor, 94
hidden agenda, 129, 160–1
Hillary, Sir Edmund, 94
history-tellers, 34
Hitchcock, Alfred, 42–3
   Psycho, 43
   Spellbound, 43
Hitler, Adolf, 102
Hofstede, Geert, 109, 110–11
   dimensions of culture, 110–11
Hogan, Christine, 149–51
Homer, 12, 57, 95
   Iliad, 12, 57
   Odyssey, 12, 57, 95
Horatius, 83
humour, 6, 17–20
   company names, 19
   jokes, 18, 39, 42, 121
   unintentional, 19
Hunt, Geoff, 92
Hunt, J. G., 144

Iacocca, Lee, 60
improvisation, 174
Indiana Jones, 92, 96
individualism–collectivism, 111
information gatekeeper, 142
inspirational leaders, 142–5
Irwin, Harry, 111–12
Isaac, 83

Jacob, 81
Jacobi, J., 86
Jaffe, A., 86
JAG Electronics, 125

Jakobson, Roman, 181
James Bond (007), 92
jazz music, 174
jealousy, 84
Jensen, Arthur, 118
Jessel, George, 5
Jesus Christ, 83, 84, 99, 103
Johnson, Amy, 94
Johnson, Spencer, 6
Jung, Carl, 86, 90–1
Jupiter (*see also* Zeus), 78, 84, 89–90

Kaye, Michael, vii–viii, 34, 164, 184
Kennedy, Alan, 116
Khan, Ghengis, 102
kicking staff in the ass (KITA), 35
King Arthur of Camelot, 82, 90
King, Billie Jean, 92
King, Martin Luther, 94, 144
Kipling, Rudyard, 5
Kluckhohn, Clyde, 75

Labyrinth, 53–4, 55, 74
Laver, Rod, 92
leaders, 36, 68, 72, 81, 95
   military, 95
   strategic apex, 144
   transformational, 135, 136
   vision, 36, 67
learning, 25–6, 48
   adult, 154–7
   facilitators of, 155–6
   life-long, 4, 152, 155, 166
   on-the-job, 28, 148
   self-directed, 154–5, 166
learning organisation, 25–6, 48
legends, 9, 31
lies, 15
life script, 9, 91
Lister, Joseph, 94
logic, 17, 20–1, 180

Index

Lone Ranger, 91
Lonergan, John, 59
Luke Skywalker, 92

Macarthur, Gen. Douglas, 96, 126
McCullagh, Cassie, 9
McEnroe, John, 92
McGrath, Dennis, 25
McGregor, Douglas, 88
    Adam and Eve archetypes, 88
    Theory X, 88
McKay, Heather, 92
McKenna, John, 165
McMurray, Adela, 108
Magellan, Ferdinand, 68
managerial parables, 32–3
managing by wandering around (MBWA), 35, 64, 135
managing resistance, 153–4
manager's roles, 139–46
Mandela, Nelson, 94, 96
mapping the big picture, 28–9
March, John, 168
Marduk, 79
Margolis, Fred, 147
Maritime Services Board, 77
Martin, Joanne, 86
Marvel, Mary, 91
masculinity–femininity, 111
matricide, 80–1
meaning-making, 25–6, 36, 38, 39, 49, 143
media, 10
Medusa, 74
me-goals, 6
Mephistopheles, 84
Mercury, 86–7
metamyth, 82
metanoia, 48
metaphors, 39–42, 76, 78, 80–1, 97–104, 117, 143, 168, 173, 176–7, 181
Meyer, Fred, 125

Micah, 81
Michener, James, 57
    Hawaii, 57
    The Source, 57
Microsoft, 73
Miller, Harry M., 62
Minogue, Kylie, 97
Minos, 53–4, 74
Minotaur, 53–4, 55, 74
mission statements, 56, 140, 143
Mitchell, Margaret, 57
    Gone With The Wind, 57
Mitchell, V. F., 168
Monaghetti, Steve, 93
monster-slaying (*see also* dragon-slaying), 54, 74, 99
Montgomery, Field Marshall Bernard Law, 95, 102
Montuori, Alfonso, 174
More, Elizabeth, 111–12
Moroney, Susie, 93
Moses, 8, 81
mottoes, 65–6
Moyers, Bill, 3, 55
Muir, Frank, 175
Murdoch, Rupert, 61, 73
myth-interpretation, 67–8, 180–1, 182
myth-making, 58–60, 74, 136
    life cycle, 61–3, 74
mythology, 55, 58–60, 66
    organisational, 75–86
    primitive, 55–7, 75–86, 91
myths
    creation, 32, 75, 76–7
    four functions of primitive, 55
    keeping myths alive, 61, 63
    modern, 9
    organisational myth themes, 75–86, 173
    sources of organisational, 68–74

Naked City, 3–4

Index

Napoleon Bonaparte, 95
Narcissus, 84
National Australia Bank, 65–6
National Mutual Life Association, 65–6
Navratilova, Martina, 92
Nebuchadnezzar, 57
Nemesis, 84
nepotism, 99
New South Wales government, 65
Nightingale, Florence, 94
nirvana, 97
Noah and the Ark, 78
non-verbal behaviours, 16
non-verbal communication, 26, 38, 112, 152
Nord, W. R., 168
Norden, Dennis, 175

Odin, King of the Slain, 97
O'Donnell-Trujillo, Nick, 116–17
officialese, 68, 74, 102
Olympus, Mount, 89
organisational audits, 68, 162–3, 165–6
organisational auditors (*see also* communication auditors), 159
organisational change, 111–12, 122–37
organisational culture, 74, 108–37
    artefacts, 108–9
    building a positive culture, 117–22
    climate, 25, 158
    climate vs culture, 108
    covert culture, 15, 112, 129, 131
    diversity in the workplace, 183–4
    subcultures, 118–20, 127
    team culture, 16, 98, 100–1, 140, 141–2, 182
    types of, 112–16
    values, 64–7, 74
organisational mafia, 131
organisational politics, 15–16, 129–30
Orpheus, 84
Ouchi, William, 110

Ovid
    Metamorphoses, 84

Pacanowsky, Michael, 116–17
Packer, Kerry, 61
Paklite travel goods, 65–6
Pankhurst, Emmeline, 94
paradigm people, 59
parent-killing, 80–1
Paretsky, Sara, 92
Pasteur, Louis, 94
patricide, 80–1
Patton, Gen. George S., 95, 96, 102
Paul, the Apostle
    Letter to the Hebrews, 57
Penn, Robert, 142–3
Pepsi, 73, 184
Perkins, Kieran, 93
Persephone, 89
personal goals, 29–30
persuasion, 7, 17–21, 26, 39, 118, 144–5
Peter, Laurence, 19
Peters, Tom, 35, 107, 122–3, 125
Peterson, M. F., 144
Phantom, The, 91
political correctness, 134
politics of institutional enhancement, 15–16, 133
politics of self-interest, 15–16, 133
Postman, Neil, 132
power distance, 110
Prince Valiant, 91
prodigal son, 81
proverbs, 34–5
Purser, Ron E., 174
Pygmalion effect, 157
Pyrrha, 78, 90

quality circles, 110
quality of life, 4, 31, 111, 136, 183
questions, 162–4

Index

Quinn, Robert, 96

Rand, Ayn, 92
   Atlas Shrugged, 92
Remus, 81
Richard the Lionheart, King, 95
Rifkin, William D., 151
rituals, 63–4, 117
Roberts, Wess, 35, 81
Roddick, Anita (*see also* Body Shop), 89
Rommel, Field Marshall Erwin, 95
Romulus, 81
Rowland, Kendrith M., 61
Rucker, Linda, 142–3
rumour, 10

Sackmann, S. A., 109
sacrifice, 54, 60, 81–3
sagas, 57, 69–73, 74
St George, 79
St Michael, 79
salvation, 81–3
Sarich, Ralph, 92, 124
Satan, 84
Savery, L. K., 154
Schank, Roger C., 6
Schein, Edgar H., 109
scripts, 9, 11–12, 17, 22, 98, 143–4
Sculley, John, 73
self-talk, 181
Senge, Peter, 25, 48
serendipity, 167, 169
shadow side, 15–16, 38, 72, 112, 118, 126–32, 131–7
Shakespeare, William, 97, 172
sibling rivalry, 81, 84
Sitkin, Sim B., 86
Skase, Christopher, 62
Smith, Dick, 58
Snell, Robin, 148–9
Solzhenitsyn, Aleksandr, 94

Spreitzer, Gretchen M., 96
Stace, Doug, 183
Starr, Brenda, 91
stereotypes, 45–6
Stevenson, Robert Louis, 5–6
stories
   gauges for determining a system's culture, 30, 31
   gist of, 16–17, 48
   impromptu, 173–5
   learning tools, 28–9
   linking new to old, 40
   moral or lesson, 34, 72, 153, 180
   official vs unofficial, 13–14
   plot or storyline, 16
   private, 8, 121
   punchline, 16–17, 20, 42
   relevance to audience, 21, 39, 76, 81
   second-hand, 11–13
   shaggy dog, 43
   stories in writing, 37–8, 153, 180–1
   told face-to-face, 36–7
   untold, 9
story-listening, 26, 45–8, 73, 178, 179–80
   giving feedback, 47–8, 49, 153, 162
   non-evaluative, 45–6, 49, 162
   radar, 183, 185
   reflecting feelings (empathy), 46–7, 49, 162
story-tellers
   roles and abilities, 39–48
story-telling
   art of, 13, 138–70
   goals, 25–30
   open, 130
story-telling organisation, 23–4, 34, 49, 76
   story-telling competencies, 186
   theatre for story-telling, 171–2
strategic managers, 40
strategic thinkers, 42, 100
Superman, 57

Index

superstitious behaviour, 116
Superwoman, 91
Sydney Adventist Hospital, 140

tales, 56
Tank Girl, 91
team leader, 139–40
Technical and Further Education (TAFE), 160–1, 164
temptation, 84, 88
Tennyson, Alfred Lord, 82
   Idylls of the King, 82
Tensing (Sherpa guide), 94
Theseus, 53–4, 55
Thor, 90
Tichy, Noel M., 130, 143
Toffler, Alvin, 171, 183
Torrance, E. Paul, 176
Tracy, Dick, 91
training and development, 48
   communication through story-telling, 22
   consultants, 162–9
   managers, 147–59
transformative managers, 182–3
Truman, Harry S., 146
trustworthiness, 18

uncertainty avoidance, 111
Uris, Leon, 57
   Exodus, 57
   Mila 18, 57

Valhalla, 97
Valkyries, 97
valour, 82
values, 64–7, 107, 108–9
Van Buskirk, William, 25
Vance, Charles M., 25
vengeance, 84
Verdi, Guiseppe, 57
Virgin Music, 73
vocabulary, 116
Von Franz, M–L., 86

Wagner, Richard, 57
   Der Ring des Nibelungen, 57
warrior-king, 89–90
Waterman, Robert H., 107
Watt, Kathy, 93
Watt, Thomas, 94
Weaver, Sigourney, 91
Weick, Karl, 144
Weingartner, Charles, 132
Wolvin, A., 45

yarns, 56
Yeider, R. A., 165
yin and yang, 60
you-goals, 6–7

Zeus (*see also* Jupiter), 78, 84, 89–90
Zorba the Greek, 4
Zorro, 91